ISBN 0-8373-3949-9

C-3949   CAREER EXAMINATION SERIES

This is your
PASSBOOK® for...

Bay Constable Trainee

Test Preparation Study Guide

Questions & Answers

NLC

NATIONAL LEARNING CORPORATION

Copyright © 2015 by

National Learning Corporation

212 Michael Drive, Syosset, New York 11791

All rights reserved, including the right of reproduction in whole or in part, in any form or by any means, electronic or mechanical, including photocopying, recording, or by any information storage and retrieval system, without permission in writing from the Publisher.

(516) 921-8888
(800) 645-6337
FAX: (516) 921-8743
www.passbooks.com
sales @ passbooks.com
info @ passbooks.com

PRINTED IN THE UNITED STATES OF AMERICA

PASSBOOK®
NOTICE

This book is SOLELY intended for, is sold ONLY to, and its use is RESTRICTED to *individual*, bona fide applicants or candidates who qualify by virtue of having seriously filed applications for appropriate license, certificate, professional and/or promotional advancement, higher school matriculation, scholarship, or other legitimate requirements of educational and/or governmental authorities.

This book is NOT intended for use, class instruction, tutoring, training, duplication, copying, reprinting, excerption, or adaptation, etc., by:

(1) Other publishers

(2) Proprietors and/or Instructors of "Coaching" and/or Preparatory Courses

(3) Personnel and/or Training Divisions of commercial, industrial, and governmental organizations

(4) Schools, colleges, or universities and/or their departments and staffs, including teachers and other personnel

(5) Testing Agencies or Bureaus

(6) Study groups which seek by the purchase of a single volume to copy and/or duplicate and/or adapt this material for use by the group as a whole without having purchased individual volumes for each of the members of the group

(7) Et al.

Such persons would be in violation of appropriate Federal and State statutes.

PROVISION OF LICENSING AGREEMENTS. — Recognized educational commercial, industrial, and governmental institutions and organizations, and others legitimately engaged in educational pursuits, including training, testing, and measurement activities, may address a request for a licensing agreement to the copyright owners, who will determine whether, and under what conditions, including fees and charges, the materials in this book may be used by them. In other words, a licensing facility exists for the legitimate use of the material in this book on other than an individual basis. However, it is asseverated and affirmed here that the material in this book *CANNOT* be used without the receipt of the express permission of such a licensing agreement from the Publishers.

NATIONAL LEARNING CORPORATION
212 Michael Drive
Syosset, New York 11791

Inquiries re licensing agreements should be addressed to:
The President
National Learning Corporation
212 Michael Drive
Syosset, New York 11791

PASSBOOK® SERIES

THE *PASSBOOK® SERIES* has been created to prepare applicants and candidates for the ultimate academic battlefield – the examination room.

At some time in our lives, each and every one of us may be required to take an examination – for validation, matriculation, admission, qualification, registration, certification, or licensure.

Based on the assumption that every applicant or candidate has met the basic formal educational standards, has taken the required number of courses, and read the necessary texts, the *PASSBOOK® SERIES* furnishes the one special preparation which may assure passing with confidence, instead of failing with insecurity. Examination questions – together with answers – are furnished as the basic vehicle for study so that the mysteries of the examination and its compounding difficulties may be eliminated or diminished by a sure method.

This book is meant to help you pass your examination provided that you qualify and are serious in your objective.

The entire field is reviewed through the huge store of content information which is succinctly presented through a provocative and challenging approach – the question-and-answer method.

A climate of success is established by furnishing the correct answers at the end of each test.

You soon learn to recognize types of questions, forms of questions, and patterns of questioning. You may even begin to anticipate expected outcomes.

You perceive that many questions are repeated or adapted so that you can gain acute insights, which may enable you to score many sure points.

You learn how to confront new questions, or types of questions, and to attack them confidently and work out the correct answers.

You note objectives and emphases, and recognize pitfalls and dangers, so that you may make positive educational adjustments.

Moreover, you are kept fully informed in relation to new concepts, methods, practices, and directions in the field.

You discover that you are actually taking the examination all the time: you are preparing for the examination by "taking" an examination, not by reading extraneous and/or supererogatory textbooks.

In short, this PASSBOOK®, used directedly, should be an important factor in helping you to pass your test.

BAY CONSTABLE TRAINEE

DUTIES
Undergoes training and assists in work involving the area patrol necessary to the enforcement of laws and codes governing boat traffic, fishing, hunting, shellfishing, conservation, structures in waterways, pollution and such other activities as come under jurisdiction of the Department of Conservation and Waterways. Performs related duties as required.

SCOPE OF THE EXAMINATION
The <u>written</u> test will cover knowledge, skills and/or abilities in such areas as:

1. Educating and interacting with the public;
2. Preparing written material; and
3. Understanding and interpreting written material.

BAY CONSTABLE TRAINEE

SAMPLE TEST QUESTIONS

THIS TEST IS IN FOUR PARTS, WITH DIRECTIONS CLEARLY EXPLAINED AT THE BEGINNING OF EACH PART.

PART I.

DIRECTIONS: You are given a set of rules, regulations or other written information which you must read. You are then required to answer a question based upon your application of the rule to a situation.

> RULE: Patrol vehicles should be checked at the start of each shift. Do not assume that the vehicle is in satisfactory condition. Check all of the lighting equipment, all emergency equipment, siren, engine, oil, transmission fluid, battery, radiator and gasoline levels, tire pressure and condition (including spare), lug wrench, jack, windshield wipers and windshield washer fluid level. Check the body of the vehicle for damaged or missing parts and report any problems, damage or discrepancies to your supervisor. At the end of your shift, leave the vehicle in optimum condition for emergency use by the next officer.

> SITUATION: Officer Burton is about to begin her patrol shift when she discovers that her police vehicle has a large dent in the left rear bumper. She knows that the vehicle did not have this dent yesterday, when she last drove it.

1. According to the Rule above, Officer Burton should most properly

   A. request that she be assigned a different vehicle
   B. begin her shift and be alert to any operating problems
   C. find out what other officers have used the vehicle since her last shift
   D. inform her supervisor about the dented bumper

PART II. PREPARING WRITTEN MATERIAL IN A POLICE SETTING: These questions test for the ability to prepare the types of reports that police officers write. You are presented with a page of notes followed by several questions. Each question consists of four restatements of the information given in the notes. From each set of four, you must choose the version that presents the information most clearly and accurately.

DIRECTIONS: You must determine which one of the choices presents all the information from a particular portion of the notes and whether the phrasing and the punctuation of the sentence(s) results in a clear and accurate presentation of the information.

2. The following is a portion of the notes you took about an accident you were dispatched to.

NOTES: Responded to a call from 26 Arbor Ave. Residence of Tessa and John Wynter. Pulled in driveway. Saw woman on Wynters' porch. Identified herself as Mrs. Orvis, a neighbor.

Which one of the choices that follow expresses the facts presented in the notes?

- A. I responded to a call from 26 Arbor Avenue, the residence of Tessa and John Wynter. When I pulled into the driveway, I saw a woman on their porch. She identified herself as Mrs. Orvis, a neighbor.

- B. Responding to a call from 26 Arbor Avenue, the residence of Tessa and John Wynter, and pulling into the driveway, I saw a neighbor on their porch, who identified herself as Mrs. Orvis.

- C. When I responded to a call from 26 Arbor Avenue, the residence of Tessa and John Wynter, I saw pulling into their driveway a woman on their porch who identified herself as Mrs. Orvis, a neighbor.

- D. Responding to a call from 26 Arbor Avenue, I saw a woman on the porch of Tessa and John Wynter's residence. She identified herself as Mrs. Orvis, a neighbor.

PART III. READING, UNDERSTANDING AND INTERPRETING WRITTEN INFORMATION: These questions test for the ability to read, understand, and interpret the kinds of written information that police officers are required to read during their formal training period and on the job.

DIRECTIONS: You are provided with brief reading selections and asked questions relating to the selections. All the information required to answer the questions is provided in the selections; you are not required to have any specific knowledge of the content areas covered in the selections.

3. "The increasing demands upon our highways from a growing population, and the development of forms of transportation not anticipated when the highways were first built have brought about congestion, confusion, and conflict, until the yearly toll of traffic accidents is now at an appalling level. If the death and disaster that traffic accidents bring throughout the year were concentrated into one calamity, we would shudder at the tremendous catastrophe. The loss is no less catastrophic because it is spread out over time and space."

Which one of the following statements concerning the yearly toll of traffic accidents is supported by the above selection?

- A. It is increasing the demands for safer means of transportation.
- B. It has resulted in increased congestion, confusion, and conflict on our highways.

C. It does not shock us as much as it should because the accidents do not all occur together.
D. It has resulted mainly from the new forms of transportation.

PART IV. MEMORY FOR FACTS AND INFORMATION: These questions test how well you can remember facts and information presented in written form after you have been given a period to read and study the information.

DIRECTIONS: You are first given a Memory Test Booklet containing a story. It will be considerably longer than the one presented here. You will have a limited period of time in which to study the details contained in the story. You will NOT be allowed to take notes while studying the story. At the end of the study period, the monitor will collect the test booklets containing the story and then hand out the test booklets containing the test questions. The first group of questions in this test booklet will ask you to recall the facts and information presented in the Memory Story.

MEMORY STORY: Officer Gary Hanson of the Burke Police Department was questioning Mathew Meyers, the owner of Meyers Sporting Goods, located at 321 Payne Avenue about a burglary that occurred the previous evening. Meyers said that when he arrived at the store at 8:50 A.M., he noticed that the rear door had been broken into. Meyers said that, after he had checked his inventory, he was missing 20 rifles, 16 pellet guns, 12 shotguns and 8 pistols.

4. How many shotguns did Meyers tell the Officer were missing from his store?

A. 8
B. 12
C. 16
D. 20

KEY (CORRECT ANSWERS)

1. D

SOLUTION: The situation states that Officer Burton has discovered a dent in the bumper of her patrol vehicle that did not exist when she last used it. The question asks what she should do about it. To answer the question, evaluate all of the choices.

Choice A states that the officer should request a different vehicle. There is nothing in the rule that states that the officer should do this. Choice A is incorrect.

Choice B states that the officer should begin her shift and be alert to any operating problems. The rule states that the officer should report any problems with the vehicle to her supervisor. Choice B is incorrect.

Choice C states that the officer should find out what other officers have used the vehicle since her last shift. There is nothing in the rule that states that the officer should do this. Choice C is incorrect.

Choice D states that the officer should inform her supervisor about the damaged bumper. This is in conformance to the rule that states that the officer should report any damaged or missing parts to her supervisor. Choice D is therefore the correct answer.

2. A

SOLUTION: To answer this question, evaluate all the choices.

Choice A: This is the only choice in which all the information is presented, and it is presented in the correct sequence. It says that the officer responded to a call from the Wynter residence, that he pulled into the driveway, saw a woman on the porch who told him her name and that she is a neighbor.

Choice B: "I saw a neighbor on their porch" suggests that the officer knew that it was a neighbor on the porch before Mrs. Orvis told him who she was. In the notes and in choice A, the woman tells him both her name and that she is a neighbor. This choice is incorrect.

Choice C: "I saw pulling into the driveway a woman on their porch" does not make sense, the woman could not be doing both. For C to be correctly written, there should be a period after Wynter, and the next sentence should begin "Pulling into the driveway, I saw…" This choice is incorrect.

Choice D: The choice does not say that 26 Arbor Avenue is the Wynters' residence. It could be the address that the call came from. Also, another piece of information is missing; the officer does not say that he pulled into the driveway. In police writing every detail is important. This choice is incorrect.

3. C

SOLUTION: To answer this question, evaluate all the choices.

Choice A: Nowhere is the passage does it say that there has been any demand for safer means of transportation. Someone who picks this choice may believe that there could or should be a demand for safer transportation, but there is nothing in the passage to base it on. This choice is incorrect.

Choice B: The passage states that it is the congestion, confusion, and conflict which results in the high toll of traffic accidents and not the other way around. A person who picks this choice could either be confused as to which is the cause and which the effect or not have read the choice carefully. This choice is incorrect.

Choice C: This choice is based on the last two sentences in the passage. The writer says "If ..., we would shudder." (A shudder is a response to shock.) The implication is that we don't, and we don't because accidents do not all occur at the same time and place. The writer then points out that we should think of the yearly toll as being catastrophic (shocking) even thought the accidents are spread out over time and space. This choice is the only correct choice.

Choice D: There are two reasons given in the paragraph for the high accident rate. One is the development of new forms of transportation; the other is the increased highway use from a growing population. Neither one is described as the main reason. It is clearly incorrect to say that the new forms of transportation are the main reason. This choice is incorrect.

4. B

SOLUTION: The question asks how many shotguns did Meyers tell the Officer were missing from his store. The last sentence in the Memory Story states, "...Meyers said that ... he was missing 20 rifles, 16 pellet guns, 12 shotguns and 8 pistols." Choice A (8) is the number of missing pistols. Choice B (12) is the correct answer. Choice C (16) is the number of missing pellet guns. Choice D (20) is the number of missing rifles.

HOW TO TAKE A TEST

I. YOU MUST PASS AN EXAMINATION

A. WHAT EVERY CANDIDATE SHOULD KNOW

Examination applicants often ask us for help in preparing for the written test. What can I study in advance? What kinds of questions will be asked? How will the test be given? How will the papers be graded?

As an applicant for a civil service examination, you may be wondering about some of these things. Our purpose here is to suggest effective methods of advance study and to describe civil service examinations.

Your chances for success on this examination can be increased if you know how to prepare. Those "pre-examination jitters" can be reduced if you know what to expect. You can even experience an adventure in good citizenship if you know why civil service exams are given.

B. WHY ARE CIVIL SERVICE EXAMINATIONS GIVEN?

Civil service examinations are important to you in two ways. As a citizen, you want public jobs filled by employees who know how to do their work. As a job seeker, you want a fair chance to compete for that job on an equal footing with other candidates. The best-known means of accomplishing this two-fold goal is the competitive examination.

Exams are widely publicized throughout the nation. They may be administered for jobs in federal, state, city, municipal, town or village governments or agencies.

Any citizen may apply, with some limitations, such as the age or residence of applicants. Your experience and education may be reviewed to see whether you meet the requirements for the particular examination. When these requirements exist, they are reasonable and applied consistently to all applicants. Thus, a competitive examination may cause you some uneasiness now, but it is your privilege and safeguard.

C. HOW ARE CIVIL SERVICE EXAMS DEVELOPED?

Examinations are carefully written by trained technicians who are specialists in the field known as "psychological measurement," in consultation with recognized authorities in the field of work that the test will cover. These experts recommend the subject matter areas or skills to be tested; only those knowledges or skills important to your success on the job are included. The most reliable books and source materials available are used as references. Together, the experts and technicians judge the difficulty level of the questions.

Test technicians know how to phrase questions so that the problem is clearly stated. Their ethics do not permit "trick" or "catch" questions. Questions may have been tried out on sample groups, or subjected to statistical analysis, to determine their usefulness.

Written tests are often used in combination with performance tests, ratings of training and experience, and oral interviews. All of these measures combine to form the best-known means of finding the right person for the right job.

II. HOW TO PASS THE WRITTEN TEST

A. NATURE OF THE EXAMINATION

To prepare intelligently for civil service examinations, you should know how they differ from school examinations you have taken. In school you were assigned certain definite pages to read or subjects to cover. The examination questions were quite detailed and usually emphasized memory. Civil service exams, on the other hand, try to discover your present ability to perform the duties of a position, plus your potentiality to learn these duties. In other words, a civil service exam attempts to predict how successful you will be. Questions cover such a broad area that they cannot be as minute and detailed as school exam questions.

In the public service similar kinds of work, or positions, are grouped together in one "class." This process is known as *position-classification*. All the positions in a class are paid according to the salary range for that class. One class title covers all of these positions, and they are all tested by the same examination.

B. FOUR BASIC STEPS

1) Study the announcement

How, then, can you know what subjects to study? Our best answer is: "Learn as much as possible about the class of positions for which you've applied." The exam will test the knowledge, skills and abilities needed to do the work.

Your most valuable source of information about the position you want is the official exam announcement. This announcement lists the training and experience qualifications. Check these standards and apply only if you come reasonably close to meeting them.

The brief description of the position in the examination announcement offers some clues to the subjects which will be tested. Think about the job itself. Review the duties in your mind. Can you perform them, or are there some in which you are rusty? Fill in the blank spots in your preparation.

Many jurisdictions preview the written test in the exam announcement by including a section called "Knowledge and Abilities Required," "Scope of the Examination," or some similar heading. Here you will find out specifically what fields will be tested.

2) Review your own background

Once you learn in general what the position is all about, and what you need to know to do the work, ask yourself which subjects you already know fairly well and which need improvement. You may wonder whether to concentrate on improving your strong areas or on building some background in your fields of weakness. When the announcement has specified "some knowledge" or "considerable knowledge," or has used adjectives like "beginning principles of…" or "advanced … methods," you can get a clue as to the number and difficulty of questions to be asked in any given field. More questions, and hence broader coverage, would be included for those subjects which are more important in the work. Now weigh your strengths and weaknesses against the job requirements and prepare accordingly.

3) Determine the level of the position

Another way to tell how intensively you should prepare is to understand the level of the job for which you are applying. Is it the entering level? In other words, is this the position in which beginners in a field of work are hired? Or is it an intermediate or advanced level? Sometimes this is indicated by such words as "Junior" or "Senior" in the class title. Other jurisdictions use Roman numerals to designate the level – Clerk I, Clerk II, for example. The word "Supervisor" sometimes appears in the title. If the level is not indicated by the title, check the description of duties. Will you be working under very close supervision, or will you have responsibility for independent decisions in this work?

4) Choose appropriate study materials

Now that you know the subjects to be examined and the relative amount of each subject to be covered, you can choose suitable study materials. For beginning level jobs, or even advanced ones, if you have a pronounced weakness in some aspect of your training, read a modern, standard textbook in that field. Be sure it is up to date and has general coverage. Such books are normally available at your library, and the librarian will be glad to help you locate one. For entry-level positions, questions of appropriate difficulty are chosen – neither highly advanced questions, nor those too simple. Such questions require careful thought but not advanced training.

If the position for which you are applying is technical or advanced, you will read more advanced, specialized material. If you are already familiar with the basic principles of your field, elementary textbooks would waste your time. Concentrate on advanced textbooks and technical periodicals. Think through the concepts and review difficult problems in your field.

These are all general sources. You can get more ideas on your own initiative, following these leads. For example, training manuals and publications of the government agency which employs workers in your field can be useful, particularly for technical and professional positions. A letter or visit to the government department involved may result in more specific study suggestions, and certainly will provide you with a more definite idea of the exact nature of the position you are seeking.

III. KINDS OF TESTS

Tests are used for purposes other than measuring knowledge and ability to perform specified duties. For some positions, it is equally important to test ability to make adjustments to new situations or to profit from training. In others, basic mental abilities not dependent on information are essential. Questions which test these things may not appear as pertinent to the duties of the position as those which test for knowledge and information. Yet they are often highly important parts of a fair examination. For very general questions, it is almost impossible to help you direct your study efforts. What we can do is to point out some of the more common of these general abilities needed in public service positions and describe some typical questions.

1) General information

Broad, general information has been found useful for predicting job success in some kinds of work. This is tested in a variety of ways, from vocabulary lists to questions about current events. Basic background in some field of work, such as sociology or economics, may be sampled in a group of questions. Often these are principles which have become familiar to most persons through exposure rather than through formal training. It is difficult to advise you how to study for these questions; being alert to the world around you is our best suggestion.

2) Verbal ability

An example of an ability needed in many positions is verbal or language ability. Verbal ability is, in brief, the ability to use and understand words. Vocabulary and grammar tests are typical measures of this ability. Reading comprehension or paragraph interpretation questions are common in many kinds of civil service tests. You are given a paragraph of written material and asked to find its central meaning.

3) Numerical ability

Number skills can be tested by the familiar arithmetic problem, by checking paired lists of numbers to see which are alike and which are different, or by interpreting charts and graphs. In the latter test, a graph may be printed in the test booklet which you are asked to use as the basis for answering questions.

4) Observation

A popular test for law-enforcement positions is the observation test. A picture is shown to you for several minutes, then taken away. Questions about the picture test your ability to observe both details and larger elements.

5) Following directions

In many positions in the public service, the employee must be able to carry out written instructions dependably and accurately. You may be given a chart with several columns, each column listing a variety of information. The questions require you to carry out directions involving the information given in the chart.

6) Skills and aptitudes

Performance tests effectively measure some manual skills and aptitudes. When the skill is one in which you are trained, such as typing or shorthand, you can practice. These tests are often very much like those given in business school or high school courses. For many of the other skills and aptitudes, however, no short-time preparation can be made. Skills and abilities natural to you or that you have developed throughout your lifetime are being tested.

Many of the general questions just described provide all the data needed to answer the questions and ask you to use your reasoning ability to find the answers. Your best preparation for these tests, as well as for tests of facts and ideas, is to be at your physical and mental best. You, no doubt, have your own methods of getting into an exam-taking mood and keeping "in shape." The next section lists some ideas on this subject.

IV. KINDS OF QUESTIONS

Only rarely is the "essay" question, which you answer in narrative form, used in civil service tests. Civil service tests are usually of the short-answer type. Full instructions for answering these questions will be given to you at the examination. But in case this is your first experience with short-answer questions and separate answer sheets, here is what you need to know:

1) Multiple-choice Questions

Most popular of the short-answer questions is the "multiple choice" or "best answer" question. It can be used, for example, to test for factual knowledge, ability to solve problems or judgment in meeting situations found at work.

A multiple-choice question is normally one of three types—
- It can begin with an incomplete statement followed by several possible endings. You are to find the one ending which *best* completes the statement, although some of the others may not be entirely wrong.
- It can also be a complete statement in the form of a question which is answered by choosing one of the statements listed.

- It can be in the form of a problem – again you select the best answer.

Here is an example of a multiple-choice question with a discussion which should give you some clues as to the method for choosing the right answer:

When an employee has a complaint about his assignment, the action which will *best* help him overcome his difficulty is to
    A. discuss his difficulty with his coworkers
    B. take the problem to the head of the organization
    C. take the problem to the person who gave him the assignment
    D. say nothing to anyone about his complaint

In answering this question, you should study each of the choices to find which is best. Consider choice "A" – Certainly an employee may discuss his complaint with fellow employees, but no change or improvement can result, and the complaint remains unresolved. Choice "B" is a poor choice since the head of the organization probably does not know what assignment you have been given, and taking your problem to him is known as "going over the head" of the supervisor. The supervisor, or person who made the assignment, is the person who can clarify it or correct any injustice. Choice "C" is, therefore, correct. To say nothing, as in choice "D," is unwise. Supervisors have and interest in knowing the problems employees are facing, and the employee is seeking a solution to his problem.

2) True/False Questions

The "true/false" or "right/wrong" form of question is sometimes used. Here a complete statement is given. Your job is to decide whether the statement is right or wrong.

SAMPLE: A roaming cell-phone call to a nearby city costs less than a non-roaming call to a distant city.

This statement is wrong, or false, since roaming calls are more expensive.
This is not a complete list of all possible question forms, although most of the others are variations of these common types. You will always get complete directions for answering questions. Be sure you understand *how* to mark your answers – ask questions until you do.

V. RECORDING YOUR ANSWERS

Computer terminals are used more and more today for many different kinds of exams.
For an examination with very few applicants, you may be told to record your answers in the test booklet itself. Separate answer sheets are much more common. If this separate answer sheet is to be scored by machine – and this is often the case – it is highly important that you mark your answers correctly in order to get credit.
An electronic scoring machine is often used in civil service offices because of the speed with which papers can be scored. Machine-scored answer sheets must be marked with a pencil, which will be given to you. This pencil has a high graphite content which responds to the electronic scoring machine. As a matter of fact, stray dots may register as answers, so do not let your pencil rest on the answer sheet while you are pondering the correct answer. Also, if your pencil lead breaks or is otherwise defective, ask for another.

Since the answer sheet will be dropped in a slot in the scoring machine, be careful not to bend the corners or get the paper crumpled.

The answer sheet normally has five vertical columns of numbers, with 30 numbers to a column. These numbers correspond to the question numbers in your test booklet. After each number, going across the page are four or five pairs of dotted lines. These short dotted lines have small letters or numbers above them. The first two pairs may also have a "T" or "F" above the letters. This indicates that the first two pairs only are to be used if the questions are of the true-false type. If the questions are multiple choice, disregard the "T" and "F" and pay attention only to the small letters or numbers.

Answer your questions in the manner of the sample that follows:

32. The largest city in the United States is
    A. Washington, D.C.
    B. New York City
    C. Chicago
    D. Detroit
    E. San Francisco

1) Choose the answer you think is best. (New York City is the largest, so "B" is correct.)
2) Find the row of dotted lines numbered the same as the question you are answering. (Find row number 32)
3) Find the pair of dotted lines corresponding to the answer. (Find the pair of lines under the mark "B.")
4) Make a solid black mark between the dotted lines.

VI. BEFORE THE TEST

Common sense will help you find procedures to follow to get ready for an examination. Too many of us, however, overlook these sensible measures. Indeed, nervousness and fatigue have been found to be the most serious reasons why applicants fail to do their best on civil service tests. Here is a list of reminders:

- Begin your preparation early – Don't wait until the last minute to go scurrying around for books and materials or to find out what the position is all about.
- Prepare continuously – An hour a night for a week is better than an all-night cram session. This has been definitely established. What is more, a night a week for a month will return better dividends than crowding your study into a shorter period of time.
- Locate the place of the exam – You have been sent a notice telling you when and where to report for the examination. If the location is in a different town or otherwise unfamiliar to you, it would be well to inquire the best route and learn something about the building.
- Relax the night before the test – Allow your mind to rest. Do not study at all that night. Plan some mild recreation or diversion; then go to bed early and get a good night's sleep.
- Get up early enough to make a leisurely trip to the place for the test – This way unforeseen events, traffic snarls, unfamiliar buildings, etc. will not upset you.
- Dress comfortably – A written test is not a fashion show. You will be known by number and not by name, so wear something comfortable.

- Leave excess paraphernalia at home – Shopping bags and odd bundles will get in your way. You need bring only the items mentioned in the official notice you received; usually everything you need is provided. Do not bring reference books to the exam. They will only confuse those last minutes and be taken away from you when in the test room.
- Arrive somewhat ahead of time – If because of transportation schedules you must get there very early, bring a newspaper or magazine to take your mind off yourself while waiting.
- Locate the examination room – When you have found the proper room, you will be directed to the seat or part of the room where you will sit. Sometimes you are given a sheet of instructions to read while you are waiting. Do not fill out any forms until you are told to do so; just read them and be prepared.
- Relax and prepare to listen to the instructions
- If you have any physical problem that may keep you from doing your best, be sure to tell the test administrator. If you are sick or in poor health, you really cannot do your best on the exam. You can come back and take the test some other time.

VII. AT THE TEST

The day of the test is here and you have the test booklet in your hand. The temptation to get going is very strong. Caution! There is more to success than knowing the right answers. You must know how to identify your papers and understand variations in the type of short-answer question used in this particular examination. Follow these suggestions for maximum results from your efforts:

1) Cooperate with the monitor
The test administrator has a duty to create a situation in which you can be as much at ease as possible. He will give instructions, tell you when to begin, check to see that you are marking your answer sheet correctly, and so on. He is not there to guard you, although he will see that your competitors do not take unfair advantage. He wants to help you do your best.

2) Listen to all instructions
Don't jump the gun! Wait until you understand all directions. In most civil service tests you get more time than you need to answer the questions. So don't be in a hurry. Read each word of instructions until you clearly understand the meaning. Study the examples, listen to all announcements and follow directions. Ask questions if you do not understand what to do.

3) Identify your papers
Civil service exams are usually identified by number only. You will be assigned a number; you must not put your name on your test papers. Be sure to copy your number correctly. Since more than one exam may be given, copy your exact examination title.

4) Plan your time
Unless you are told that a test is a "speed" or "rate of work" test, speed itself is usually not important. Time enough to answer all the questions will be provided, but this does not mean that you have all day. An overall time limit has been set. Divide the total time (in minutes) by the number of questions to determine the approximate time you have for each question.

5) Do not linger over difficult questions

If you come across a difficult question, mark it with a paper clip (useful to have along) and come back to it when you have been through the booklet. One caution if you do this – be sure to skip a number on your answer sheet as well. Check often to be sure that you have not lost your place and that you are marking in the row numbered the same as the question you are answering.

6) Read the questions

Be sure you know what the question asks! Many capable people are unsuccessful because they failed to *read* the questions correctly.

7) Answer all questions

Unless you have been instructed that a penalty will be deducted for incorrect answers, it is better to guess than to omit a question.

8) Speed tests

It is often better NOT to guess on speed tests. It has been found that on timed tests people are tempted to spend the last few seconds before time is called in marking answers at random – without even reading them – in the hope of picking up a few extra points. To discourage this practice, the instructions may warn you that your score will be "corrected" for guessing. That is, a penalty will be applied. The incorrect answers will be deducted from the correct ones, or some other penalty formula will be used.

9) Review your answers

If you finish before time is called, go back to the questions you guessed or omitted to give them further thought. Review other answers if you have time.

10) Return your test materials

If you are ready to leave before others have finished or time is called, take ALL your materials to the monitor and leave quietly. Never take any test material with you. The monitor can discover whose papers are not complete, and taking a test booklet may be grounds for disqualification.

VIII. EXAMINATION TECHNIQUES

1) Read the general instructions carefully. These are usually printed on the first page of the exam booklet. As a rule, these instructions refer to the timing of the examination; the fact that you should not start work until the signal and must stop work at a signal, etc. If there are any *special* instructions, such as a choice of questions to be answered, make sure that you note this instruction carefully.

2) When you are ready to start work on the examination, that is as soon as the signal has been given, read the instructions to each question booklet, underline any key words or phrases, such as *least, best, outline, describe* and the like. In this way you will tend to answer as requested rather than discover on reviewing your paper that you *listed without describing*, that you selected the *worst* choice rather than the *best* choice, etc.

3) If the examination is of the objective or multiple-choice type – that is, each question will also give a series of possible answers: A, B, C or D, and you are called upon to select the best answer and write the letter next to that answer on your answer paper – it is advisable to start answering each question in turn. There may be anywhere from 50 to 100 such questions in the three or four hours allotted and you can see how much time would be taken if you read through all the questions before beginning to answer any. Furthermore, if you come across a question or group of questions which you know would be difficult to answer, it would undoubtedly affect your handling of all the other questions.

4) If the examination is of the essay type and contains but a few questions, it is a moot point as to whether you should read all the questions before starting to answer any one. Of course, if you are given a choice – say five out of seven and the like – then it is essential to read all the questions so you can eliminate the two that are most difficult. If, however, you are asked to answer all the questions, there may be danger in trying to answer the easiest one first because you may find that you will spend too much time on it. The best technique is to answer the first question, then proceed to the second, etc.

5) Time your answers. Before the exam begins, write down the time it started, then add the time allowed for the examination and write down the time it must be completed, then divide the time available somewhat as follows:
    - If 3-1/2 hours are allowed, that would be 210 minutes. If you have 80 objective-type questions, that would be an average of 2-1/2 minutes per question. Allow yourself no more than 2 minutes per question, or a total of 160 minutes, which will permit about 50 minutes to review.
    - If for the time allotment of 210 minutes there are 7 essay questions to answer, that would average about 30 minutes a question. Give yourself only 25 minutes per question so that you have about 35 minutes to review.

6) The most important instruction is to *read each question* and make sure you know what is wanted. The second most important instruction is to *time yourself properly* so that you answer every question. The third most important instruction is to *answer every question*. Guess if you have to but include something for each question. Remember that you will receive no credit for a blank and will probably receive some credit if you write something in answer to an essay question. If you guess a letter – say "B" for a multiple-choice question – you may have guessed right. If you leave a blank as an answer to a multiple-choice question, the examiners may respect your feelings but it will not add a point to your score. Some exams may penalize you for wrong answers, so in such cases *only*, you may not want to guess unless you have some basis for your answer.

7) Suggestions
    a. Objective-type questions
        1. Examine the question booklet for proper sequence of pages and questions
        2. Read all instructions carefully
        3. Skip any question which seems too difficult; return to it after all other questions have been answered
        4. Apportion your time properly; do not spend too much time on any single question or group of questions

5. Note and underline key words – *all, most, fewest, least, best, worst, same, opposite,* etc.
6. Pay particular attention to negatives
7. Note unusual option, e.g., unduly long, short, complex, different or similar in content to the body of the question
8. Observe the use of "hedging" words – *probably, may, most likely,* etc.
9. Make sure that your answer is put next to the same number as the question
10. Do not second-guess unless you have good reason to believe the second answer is definitely more correct
11. Cross out original answer if you decide another answer is more accurate; do not erase until you are ready to hand your paper in
12. Answer all questions; guess unless instructed otherwise
13. Leave time for review

b. Essay questions
1. Read each question carefully
2. Determine exactly what is wanted. Underline key words or phrases.
3. Decide on outline or paragraph answer
4. Include many different points and elements unless asked to develop any one or two points or elements
5. Show impartiality by giving pros and cons unless directed to select one side only
6. Make and write down any assumptions you find necessary to answer the questions
7. Watch your English, grammar, punctuation and choice of words
8. Time your answers; don't crowd material

8) Answering the essay question

Most essay questions can be answered by framing the specific response around several key words or ideas. Here are a few such key words or ideas:

M's: manpower, materials, methods, money, management
P's: purpose, program, policy, plan, procedure, practice, problems, pitfalls, personnel, public relations

a. Six basic steps in handling problems:
1. Preliminary plan and background development
2. Collect information, data and facts
3. Analyze and interpret information, data and facts
4. Analyze and develop solutions as well as make recommendations
5. Prepare report and sell recommendations
6. Install recommendations and follow up effectiveness

b. Pitfalls to avoid
1. *Taking things for granted* – A statement of the situation does not necessarily imply that each of the elements is necessarily true; for example, a complaint may be invalid and biased so that all that can be taken for granted is that a complaint has been registered

2. *Considering only one side of a situation* – Wherever possible, indicate several alternatives and then point out the reasons you selected the best one
3. *Failing to indicate follow up* – Whenever your answer indicates action on your part, make certain that you will take proper follow-up action to see how successful your recommendations, procedures or actions turn out to be
4. *Taking too long in answering any single question* – Remember to time your answers properly

IX. AFTER THE TEST

Scoring procedures differ in detail among civil service jurisdictions although the general principles are the same. Whether the papers are hand-scored or graded by machine we have described, they are nearly always graded by number. That is, the person who marks the paper knows only the number – never the name – of the applicant. Not until all the papers have been graded will they be matched with names. If other tests, such as training and experience or oral interview ratings have been given, scores will be combined. Different parts of the examination usually have different weights. For example, the written test might count 60 percent of the final grade, and a rating of training and experience 40 percent. In many jurisdictions, veterans will have a certain number of points added to their grades.

After the final grade has been determined, the names are placed in grade order and an eligible list is established. There are various methods for resolving ties between those who get the same final grade – probably the most common is to place first the name of the person whose application was received first. Job offers are made from the eligible list in the order the names appear on it. You will be notified of your grade and your rank as soon as all these computations have been made. This will be done as rapidly as possible.

People who are found to meet the requirements in the announcement are called "eligibles." Their names are put on a list of eligible candidates. An eligible's chances of getting a job depend on how high he stands on this list and how fast agencies are filling jobs from the list.

When a job is to be filled from a list of eligibles, the agency asks for the names of people on the list of eligibles for that job. When the civil service commission receives this request, it sends to the agency the names of the three people highest on this list. Or, if the job to be filled has specialized requirements, the office sends the agency the names of the top three persons who meet these requirements from the general list.

The appointing officer makes a choice from among the three people whose names were sent to him. If the selected person accepts the appointment, the names of the others are put back on the list to be considered for future openings.

That is the rule in hiring from all kinds of eligible lists, whether they are for typist, carpenter, chemist, or something else. For every vacancy, the appointing officer has his choice of any one of the top three eligibles on the list. This explains why the person whose name is on top of the list sometimes does not get an appointment when some of the persons lower on the list do. If the appointing officer chooses the second or third eligible, the No. 1 eligible does not get a job at once, but stays on the list until he is appointed or the list is terminated.

X. HOW TO PASS THE INTERVIEW TEST

The examination for which you applied requires an oral interview test. You have already taken the written test and you are now being called for the interview test – the final part of the formal examination.

You may think that it is not possible to prepare for an interview test and that there are no procedures to follow during an interview. Our purpose is to point out some things you can do in advance that will help you and some good rules to follow and pitfalls to avoid while you are being interviewed.

What is an interview supposed to test?

The written examination is designed to test the technical knowledge and competence of the candidate; the oral is designed to evaluate intangible qualities, not readily measured otherwise, and to establish a list showing the relative fitness of each candidate – as measured against his competitors – for the position sought. Scoring is not on the basis of "right" and "wrong," but on a sliding scale of values ranging from "not passable" to "outstanding." As a matter of fact, it is possible to achieve a relatively low score without a single "incorrect" answer because of evident weakness in the qualities being measured.

Occasionally, an examination may consist entirely of an oral test – either an individual or a group oral. In such cases, information is sought concerning the technical knowledges and abilities of the candidate, since there has been no written examination for this purpose. More commonly, however, an oral test is used to supplement a written examination.

Who conducts interviews?

The composition of oral boards varies among different jurisdictions. In nearly all, a representative of the personnel department serves as chairman. One of the members of the board may be a representative of the department in which the candidate would work. In some cases, "outside experts" are used, and, frequently, a businessman or some other representative of the general public is asked to serve. Labor and management or other special groups may be represented. The aim is to secure the services of experts in the appropriate field.

However the board is composed, it is a good idea (and not at all improper or unethical) to ascertain in advance of the interview who the members are and what groups they represent. When you are introduced to them, you will have some idea of their backgrounds and interests, and at least you will not stutter and stammer over their names.

What should be done before the interview?

While knowledge about the board members is useful and takes some of the surprise element out of the interview, there is other preparation which is more substantive. It *is* possible to prepare for an oral interview – in several ways:

1) Keep a copy of your application and review it carefully before the interview

This may be the only document before the oral board, and the starting point of the interview. Know what education and experience you have listed there, and the sequence and dates of all of it. Sometimes the board will ask you to review the highlights of your experience for them; you should not have to hem and haw doing it.

2) Study the class specification and the examination announcement

Usually, the oral board has one or both of these to guide them. The qualities, characteristics or knowledges required by the position sought are stated in these documents. They offer valuable clues as to the nature of the oral interview. For example, if the job involves supervisory responsibilities, the announcement will usually indicate that knowledge of modern supervisory methods and the qualifications of the candidate as a supervisor will be tested. If so, you can expect such questions, frequently in the form of a hypothetical situation which you are expected to solve. NEVER go into an oral without knowledge of the duties and responsibilities of the job you seek.

3) Think through each qualification required

Try to visualize the kind of questions you would ask if you were a board member. How well could you answer them? Try especially to appraise your own knowledge and background in each area, *measured against the job sought*, and identify any areas in which you are weak. Be critical and realistic – do not flatter yourself.

4) Do some general reading in areas in which you feel you may be weak

For example, if the job involves supervision and your past experience has NOT, some general reading in supervisory methods and practices, particularly in the field of human relations, might be useful. Do NOT study agency procedures or detailed manuals. The oral board will be testing your understanding and capacity, not your memory.

5) Get a good night's sleep and watch your general health and mental attitude

You will want a clear head at the interview. Take care of a cold or any other minor ailment, and of course, no hangovers.

What should be done on the day of the interview?

Now comes the day of the interview itself. Give yourself plenty of time to get there. Plan to arrive somewhat ahead of the scheduled time, particularly if your appointment is in the fore part of the day. If a previous candidate fails to appear, the board might be ready for you a bit early. By early afternoon an oral board is almost invariably behind schedule if there are many candidates, and you may have to wait. Take along a book or magazine to read, or your application to review, but leave any extraneous material in the waiting room when you go in for your interview. In any event, relax and compose yourself.

The matter of dress is important. The board is forming impressions about you – from your experience, your manners, your attitude, and your appearance. Give your personal appearance careful attention. Dress your best, but not your flashiest. Choose conservative, appropriate clothing, and be sure it is immaculate. This is a business interview, and your appearance should indicate that you regard it as such. Besides, being well groomed and properly dressed will help boost your confidence.

Sooner or later, someone will call your name and escort you into the interview room. *This is it.* From here on you are on your own. It is too late for any more preparation. But remember, you asked for this opportunity to prove your fitness, and you are here because your request was granted.

What happens when you go in?

The usual sequence of events will be as follows: The clerk (who is often the board stenographer) will introduce you to the chairman of the oral board, who will introduce you to the other members of the board. Acknowledge the introductions before you sit down. Do not be surprised if you find a microphone facing you or a stenotypist sitting by. Oral interviews are usually recorded in the event of an appeal or other review.

Usually the chairman of the board will open the interview by reviewing the highlights of your education and work experience from your application – primarily for the benefit of the other members of the board, as well as to get the material into the record. Do not interrupt or comment unless there is an error or significant misinterpretation; if that is the case, do not hesitate. But do not quibble about insignificant matters. Also, he will usually ask you some question about your education, experience or your present job – partly to get you to start talking and to establish the interviewing "rapport." He may start the actual questioning, or turn it over to one of the other members. Frequently, each member undertakes the questioning on a particular area, one in which he is perhaps most competent, so you can expect each member to participate in the examination. Because time is limited, you may also expect some rather abrupt switches in the direction the questioning takes, so do not be upset by it. Normally, a board member will not pursue a single line of questioning unless he discovers a particular strength or weakness.

After each member has participated, the chairman will usually ask whether any member has any further questions, then will ask you if you have anything you wish to add. Unless you are expecting this question, it may floor you. Worse, it may start you off on an extended, extemporaneous speech. The board is not usually seeking more information. The question is principally to offer you a last opportunity to present further qualifications or to indicate that you have nothing to add. So, if you feel that a significant qualification or characteristic has been overlooked, it is proper to point it out in a sentence or so. Do not compliment the board on the thoroughness of their examination – they have been sketchy, and you know it. If you wish, merely say, "No thank you, I have nothing further to add." This is a point where you can "talk yourself out" of a good impression or fail to present an important bit of information. Remember, *you close the interview yourself.*

The chairman will then say, "That is all, Mr. _____, thank you." Do not be startled; the interview is over, and quicker than you think. Thank him, gather your belongings and take your leave. Save your sigh of relief for the other side of the door.

How to put your best foot forward

Throughout this entire process, you may feel that the board individually and collectively is trying to pierce your defenses, seek out your hidden weaknesses and embarrass and confuse you. Actually, this is not true. They are obliged to make an appraisal of your qualifications for the job you are seeking, and they want to see you in your best light. Remember, they must interview all candidates and a non-cooperative candidate may become a failure in spite of their best efforts to bring out his qualifications. Here are 15 suggestions that will help you:

1) Be natural – Keep your attitude confident, not cocky

If you are not confident that you can do the job, do not expect the board to be. Do not apologize for your weaknesses, try to bring out your strong points. The board is interested in a positive, not negative, presentation. Cockiness will antagonize any board member and make him wonder if you are covering up a weakness by a false show of strength.

2) Get comfortable, but don't lounge or sprawl

Sit erectly but not stiffly. A careless posture may lead the board to conclude that you are careless in other things, or at least that you are not impressed by the importance of the occasion. Either conclusion is natural, even if incorrect. Do not fuss with your clothing, a pencil or an ashtray. Your hands may occasionally be useful to emphasize a point; do not let them become a point of distraction.

3) Do not wisecrack or make small talk

This is a serious situation, and your attitude should show that you consider it as such. Further, the time of the board is limited – they do not want to waste it, and neither should you.

4) Do not exaggerate your experience or abilities

In the first place, from information in the application or other interviews and sources, the board may know more about you than you think. Secondly, you probably will not get away with it. An experienced board is rather adept at spotting such a situation, so do not take the chance.

5) If you know a board member, do not make a point of it, yet do not hide it

Certainly you are not fooling him, and probably not the other members of the board. Do not try to take advantage of your acquaintanceship – it will probably do you little good.

6) Do not dominate the interview

Let the board do that. They will give you the clues – do not assume that you have to do all the talking. Realize that the board has a number of questions to ask you, and do not try to take up all the interview time by showing off your extensive knowledge of the answer to the first one.

7) Be attentive

You only have 20 minutes or so, and you should keep your attention at its sharpest throughout. When a member is addressing a problem or question to you, give him your undivided attention. Address your reply principally to him, but do not exclude the other board members.

8) Do not interrupt

A board member may be stating a problem for you to analyze. He will ask you a question when the time comes. Let him state the problem, and wait for the question.

9) Make sure you understand the question

Do not try to answer until you are sure what the question is. If it is not clear, restate it in your own words or ask the board member to clarify it for you. However, do not haggle about minor elements.

10) Reply promptly but not hastily

A common entry on oral board rating sheets is "candidate responded readily," or "candidate hesitated in replies." Respond as promptly and quickly as you can, but do not jump to a hasty, ill-considered answer.

11) Do not be peremptory in your answers

A brief answer is proper – but do not fire your answer back. That is a losing game from your point of view. The board member can probably ask questions much faster than you can answer them.

12) Do not try to create the answer you think the board member wants

He is interested in what kind of mind you have and how it works – not in playing games. Furthermore, he can usually spot this practice and will actually grade you down on it.

13) Do not switch sides in your reply merely to agree with a board member

Frequently, a member will take a contrary position merely to draw you out and to see if you are willing and able to defend your point of view. Do not start a debate, yet do not surrender a good position. If a position is worth taking, it is worth defending.

14) Do not be afraid to admit an error in judgment if you are shown to be wrong
   The board knows that you are forced to reply without any opportunity for careful consideration. Your answer may be demonstrably wrong. If so, admit it and get on with the interview.

15) Do not dwell at length on your present job
   The opening question may relate to your present assignment. Answer the question but do not go into an extended discussion. You are being examined for a *new* job, not your present one. As a matter of fact, try to phrase ALL your answers in terms of the job for which you are being examined.

Basis of Rating
   Probably you will forget most of these "do's" and "don'ts" when you walk into the oral interview room. Even remembering them all will not ensure you a passing grade. Perhaps you did not have the qualifications in the first place. But remembering them will help you to put your best foot forward, without treading on the toes of the board members.
   Rumor and popular opinion to the contrary notwithstanding, an oral board wants you to make the best appearance possible. They know you are under pressure – but they also want to see how you respond to it as a guide to what your reaction would be under the pressures of the job you seek. They will be influenced by the degree of poise you display, the personal traits you show and the manner in which you respond.

ABOUT THIS BOOK

   This book contains tests divided into Examination Sections. Go through each test, answering every question in the margin. We have also attached a sample answer sheet at the back of the book that can be removed and used. At the end of each test look at the answer key and check your answers. On the ones you got wrong, look at the right answer choice and learn. Do not fill in the answers first. Do not memorize the questions and answers, but understand the answer and principles involved. On your test, the questions will likely be different from the samples. Questions are changed and new ones added. If you understand these past questions you should have success with any changes that arise. Tests may consist of several types of questions. We have additional books on each subject should more study be advisable or necessary for you. Finally, the more you study, the better prepared you will be. This book is intended to be the last thing you study before you walk into the examination room. Prior study of relevant texts is also recommended. NLC publishes some of these in our Fundamental Series. Knowledge and good sense are important factors in passing your exam. Good luck also helps. So now study this Passbook, absorb the material contained within and take that knowledge into the examination. Then do your best to pass that exam.

EXAMINATION SECTION

EDUCATING AND INTERACTING WITH THE PUBLIC

These questions test for knowledge of techniques used to interact effectively with individual citizens and/or community groups, to educate or inform them about topics of concern, to publicize or clarify agency programs or policies, to negotiate conflicts or resolve complaints, and to represent one's agency or program in a manner in keeping with good public relations practices. Questions may also cover interacting with others in cooperative efforts of public outreach or service. There will be 15 questions in this subject area on the written test.

TEST TASK:
You will be presented with a variety of situations in which you must apply knowledge of how best to interact with other people.

SAMPLE QUESTION:
A person approaches you expressing anger about a recent action by your department. Which one of the following should be your first response to this person?

A. Interrupt to say you cannot discuss the situation until he calms down.
B. Say you are sorry that he has been negatively affected by your department's action.
C. Listen and express understanding that he has been upset by your department's action.
D. Give him an explanation of the reasons for your department's action.

The correct answer to this sample question is choice C

C. SOLUTION:

Choice A *is not correct.* It would be inappropriate to interrupt. In addition, saying that you cannot discuss the situation until the person calms down will likely aggravate him further.

Choice B *is not correct.* Apologizing for your department's action implies that the action was improper.

Choice C is the correct answer to this question. By listening and expressing understanding that your department's action has upset him, you demonstrate that you have heard and understand his feelings and point of view.

Choice D *is not correct.* While an explanation of the reasons for the action may be appropriate at a later time, at this moment the person is angry and would not be receptive to such an explanation.

EXAMINATION SECTION
TEST 1

DIRECTIONS: Each question or incomplete statement is followed by several suggested answers or completions. Select the one that BEST answers the question or completes the statement. *PRINT THE LETTER OF THE CORRECT ANSWER IN THE SPACE AT THE RIGHT.*

1. When conducting a needs assessment for the purpose of education planning, an agency's FIRST step is to identify or provide 1.____

    A. a profile of population characteristics
    B. barriers to participation
    C. existing resources
    D. profiles of competing resources

2. Research has demonstrated that of the following, the most effective medium for communicating with external publics is/are 2.____

    A. video news releases
    B. television
    C. radio
    D. newspapers

3. Basic ideas behind the effort to influence the attitudes and behaviors of a constituency include each of the following, EXCEPT the idea that 3.____

    A. words, rather than actions or events, are most likely to motivate
    B. demands for action are a usual response
    C. self-interest usually figures heavily into public involvement
    D. the reliability of change programs is difficult to assess

4. An agency representative is trying to craft a pithy message to constituents in order to encourage the use agency program resources. Choosing an audience for such messages is easiest when the message 4.____

    A. is project- or behavior-based
    B. is combined with other messages
    C. is abstract
    D. has a broad appeal

5. Of the following factors, the most important to the success of an agency's external education or communication programs is the 5.____

    A. amount of resources used to implement them
    B. public's prior experiences with the agency
    C. real value of the program to the public
    D. commitment of the internal audience

6. A representative for a state agency is being interviewed by a reporter from a local news network. The representative is being asked to defend a program that is extremely unpopular in certain parts of the municipality. When a constituency is known to be opposed to a position, the most useful communication strategy is to present 6.____

A. only the arguments that are consistent with constituents' views
B. only the agency's side of the issue
C. both sides of the argument as clearly as possible
D. both sides of the argument, omitting key information about the opposing position

7. The most significant barriers to effective agency community relations include
   I. widespread distrust of communication strategies
   II. the media's "watchdog" stance
   III. public apathy
   IV. statutory opposition

   A. I only
   B. I and II
   C. II and III
   D. III and IV

7.____

8. In conducting an education program, many agencies use workshops and seminars in a classroom setting. Advantages of classroom-style teaching over other means of educating the public include each of the following, EXCEPT:

   A. enabling an instructor to verify learning through testing and interaction with the target audience
   B. enabling hands-on practice and other participatory learning techniques
   C. ability to reach an unlimited number of participants in a given length of time
   D. ability to convey the latest, most up-to-date information

8.____

9. The _____ model of community relations is characterized by an attempt to persuade the public to adopt the agency's point of view.

   A. two-way symmetric
   B. two-way asymmetric
   C. public information
   D. press agency/publicity

9.____

10. Important elements of an internal situation analysis include the
    I. list of agency opponents
    II. communication audit
    III. updated organizational almanac
    IV. stakeholder analysis

    A. I and II
    B. I, II and III
    C. II and III
    D. I, II, III and IV

10.____

11. Government agency information efforts typically involve each of the following objectives, EXCEPT to

    A. implement changes in the policies of government agencies to align with public opinion
    B. communicate the work of agencies
    C. explain agency techniques in a way that invites input from citizens
    D. provide citizen feedback to government administrators

11.____

12. Factors that are likely to influence the effectiveness of an educational campaign include the
    I. level of homogeneity among intended participants
    II. number and types of media used
    III. receptivity of the intended participants
    IV. level of specificity in the message or behavior to be taught

    A. I and II
    B. I, II and III
    C. II and III
    D. I, II, III and IV

13. An agency representative is writing instructional objectives that will later help to measure the effectiveness of an educational program. Which of the following verbs, included in an objective, would be MOST helpful for the purpose of measuring effectiveness?

    A. Know
    B. Identify
    C. Learn
    D. Comprehend

14. A state education agency wants to encourage participation in a program that has just received a boost through new federal legislation. The program is intended to include participants from a wide variety of socioeconomic and other demographic characteristics. The agency wants to launch a broad-based program that will inform virtually every interested party in the state about the program's new circumstances. In attempting to deliver this message to such a wide-ranging constituency, the agency's best practice would be to

    A. broadcast the same message through as many different media channels as possible
    B. focus on one discrete segment of the public at a time
    C. craft a message whose appeal is as broad as the public itself
    D. let the program's achievements speak for themselves and rely on word-of-mouth

15. Advantages associated with using the World Wide Web as an educational tool include
    I. an appeal to younger generations of the public
    II. visually-oriented, interactive learning
    III. learning that is not confined by space, time, or institutional as sociation
    IV. a variety of methods for verifying use and learning

    A. I only
    B. I and II
    C. I, II and III
    D. I, II, III and IV

16. In agencies involved in health care, community relations is a critical function because it

    A. serves as an intermediary between the agency and consumers
    B. generates a clear mission statement for agency goals and priorities
    C. ensures patient privacy while satisfying the media's right to information
    D. helps marketing professionals determine the wants and needs of agency constituents

17. After an extensive campaign to promote its newest program to constituents, an agency learns that most of the audience did not understand the intended message. Most likely, the agency has

   A. chosen words that were intended to inform, rather than persuade
   B. not accurately interpreted what the audience really needed to know
   C. overestimated the ability of the audience to receive and process the message
   D. compensated for noise that may have interrupted the message

18. The necessary elements that lead to conviction and motivation in the minds of participants in an educational or information program include each of the following, EXCEPT the _____ of the message.

   A. acceptability
   B. intensity
   C. single-channel appeal
   D. pervasiveness

19. Printed materials are often at the core of educational programs provided by public agencies. The primary disadvantage associated with print is that it

   A. does not enable comprehensive treatment of a topic
   B. is generally unreliable in term of assessing results
   C. is often the most expensive medium available
   D. is constrained by time

20. Traditional thinking on public opinion holds that there is about _____ percent of the public who are pivotal to shifting the balance and momentum of opinion—they are concerned about an issue, but not fanatical, and interested enough to pay attention to a reasoned discussion.

   A. 2
   B. 10
   C. 33
   D. 51

21. One of the most useful guidelines for influencing attitude change among people is to

   A. inviting the target audience to come to you, rather than approaching them
   B. use moral appeals as the primary approach
   C. use concrete images to enable people to see the results of behaviors or indifference
   D. offer tangible rewards to people for changes in behaviors

22. An agency is attempting to evaluate the effectiveness of its educational program. For this purpose, it wants to observe several focus groups discussing the same program. Which of the following would NOT be a guideline for the use of focus groups?

   A. Focus groups should only include those who have participated in the program.
   B. Be sure to accurately record the discussion.
   C. The same questions should be asked at each focus group meeting.
   D. It is often helpful to have a neutral, non-agency employee facilitate discussions.

23. Research consistently shows that _____ is the determinant most likely to make a newspaper editor run a news release.

    A. novelty
    B. prominence
    C. proximity
    D. conflict

24. Which of the following is NOT one of the major variables to take into account when considering a population needs assessment?

    A. State of program development
    B. Resources available
    C. Demographics
    D. Community attitudes

25. The first step in any communications audit is to

    A. develop a research instrument
    B. determine how the organization currently communicates
    C. hire a contractor
    D. determine which audience to assess

KEY (CORRECT ANSWERS)

1.	A	11.	A
2.	D	12.	D
3.	A	13.	B
4.	A	14.	B
5.	D	15.	C
6.	C	16.	A
7.	D	17.	B
8.	C	18.	C
9.	B	19.	B
10.	C	20.	B

21. C
22. A
23. C
24. C
25. D

TEST 2

DIRECTIONS: Each question or incomplete statement is followed by several suggested answers or completions. Select the one that BEST answers the question or completes the statement. *PRINT THE LETTER OF THE CORRECT ANSWER IN THE SPACE AT THE RIGHT.*

1. A public relations practitioner at an agency has just composed a press release highlighting a program's recent accomplishments and success stories. In pitching such releases to print outlets, the practitioner should
    I. e-mail, mail, or send them by messenger
    II. address them to "editor" or "news director"
    III. have an assistant call all media contacts by telephone
    IV. ask reporters or editors how they prefer to receive them

    A. I and II   B. I and IV   C. II, III and IV   D. III only

2. The "output goals" of an educational program are MOST likely to include

    A. specified ratings of services by participants on a standardized scale
    B. observable effects on a given community or clientele
    C. the number of instructional hours provided
    D. the number of participants served

3. An agency wants to evaluate satisfaction levels among program participants, and mails out questionnaires to everyone who has been enrolled in the last year. The primary problem associated with this method of evaluative research is that it

    A. poses a significant inconvenience for respondents
    B. is inordinately expensive
    C. does not allow for follow-up or clarification questions
    D. usually involves a low response rate

4. A communications audit is an important tool for measuring

    A. the depth of penetration of a particular message or program
    B. the cost of the organization's information campaigns
    C. how key audiences perceive an organization
    D. the commitment of internal stakeholders

5. The "ABC's" of written learning objectives include each of the following, EXCEPT

    A. Audience   B. Behavior   C. Conditions   D. Delineation

6. When attempting to change the behaviors of constituents, it is important to keep in mind that
    I. most people are skeptical of communications that try to get them to change their behaviors
    II. in most cases, a person selects the media to which he exposes himself
    III. people tend to react defensively to messages or programs that rely on fear as a motivating factor
    IV. programs should aim for the broadest appeal possible in order to include as many participants as possible

    A. I and II   B. I, II and III   C. II and III   D. I, II, III and IV

7. The "laws" of public opinion include the idea that it is 7.____

   A. useful for anticipating emergencies
   B. not sensitive to important events
   C. basically determined by self-interest
   D. sustainable through persistent appeals

8. Which of the following types of evaluations is used to measure public attitudes before 8.____
and after an information/educational program?

   A. retrieval study
   B. copy test
   C. quota sampling
   D. benchmark study

9. The primary source for internal communications is/are usually 9.____

   A. flow charts
   B. meetings
   C. voice mail
   D. printed publications

10. An agency representative is putting together informational materials brochures and a 10.____
newsletteroutlining changes in one of the state's biggest benefits programs. In assembling print materials as a medium for delivering information to the public, the representative should keep in mind each of the following trends:

    I. For various reasons, the reading capabilities of the public are in general decline
    II. Without tables and graphs to help illustrate the changes, it is unlikely that the message will be delivered effectively
    III. Professionals and career-oriented people are highly receptive to information written in the form of a journal article or empirical study
    IV. People tend to be put off by print materials that use itemized and bulleted (•) lists.

    A. I and II   B. I, II and III   C. II and III   D. I, II, III and IV

11. Which of the following steps in a problem-oriented information campaign would typically 11.____
be implemented FIRST?

    A. Deciding on tactics
    B. Determining a communications strategy
    C. Evaluating the problem's impact
    D. Developing an organizational strategy

12. A common pitfall in conducting an educational program is to

    A. aim it at the wrong target audience
    B. overfund it
    C. leave it in the hands of people who are in the business of education, rather than those with expertise in the business of the organization
    D. ignore the possibility that some other organization is meeting the same educational need for the target audience

13. The key factors that affect the credibility of an agency's educational program include

    A. organization
    B. scope
    C. sophistication
    D. penetration

14. Research on public opinion consistently demonstrates that it is

    A. easy to move people toward a strong opinion on anything, as long as they are approached directly through their emotions
    B. easier to move people away from an opinion they currently hold than to have them form an opinion about something they have not previously cared about
    C. easy to move people toward a strong opinion on anything, as long as the message appeals to their reason and intellect
    D. difficult to move people toward a strong opinion on anything, no matter what the approach

15. In conducting an education program, many agencies use meetings and conferences to educate an audience about the organization and its programs. Advantages associated with this approach include
    I. a captive audience that is known to be interested in the topic
    II. ample opportunities for verifying learning
    III. cost-efficient meeting space
    IV. the ability to provide information on a wider variety of subjects

    A. I and II
    B. I, III and IV
    C. II and III
    D. I, II, III and IV

16. An agency is attempting to evaluate the effectiveness of its educational programs. For this purpose, it wants to observe several focus groups discussing particular programs. For this purpose, a focus group should never number more than _____ participants.

    A. 5   B. 10   C. 15   D. 20

17. A _____ speech is written so that several agency members can deliver it to different audiences with only minor variations.

    A. basic   B. printed   C. quota   D. pattern

18. Which of the following statements about public opinion is generally considered to be FALSE?   18.____

    A. Opinion is primarily reactive rather than proactive.
    B. People have more opinions about goals than about the means by which to achieve them.
    C. Facts tend to shift opinion in the accepted direction when opinion is not solidly structured.
    D. Public opinion is based more on information than desire.

19. An agency is trying to promote its educational program. As a general rule, the agency should NOT assume that   19.____

    A. people will only participate if they perceive an individual benefit
    B. promotions need to be aimed at small, discrete groups
    C. if the program is good, the audience will find out about it
    D. a variety of methods, including advertising, special events, and direct mail, should be considered

20. In planning a successful educational program, probably the first and most important question for an agency to ask is: 20.____

    A. What will be the content of the program?
    B. Who will be served by the program?
    C. When is the best time to schedule the program?
    D. Why is the program necessary?

21. Media kits are LEAST likely to contain   21.____

    A. fact sheets
    B. memoranda
    C. photographs with captions
    D. news releases

22. The use of pamphlets and booklets as media for communication with the public often involves the disadvantage that   22.____

    A. the messages contained within them are frequently nonspecific
    B. it is difficult to measure their effectiveness in delivering the message
    C. there are few opportunities for people to refer to them
    D. color reproduction is poor

23. The most important prerequisite of a good educational program is an   23.____

    A. abundance of resources to implement it
    B. individual staff unit formed for the purpose of program delivery
    C. accurate needs assessment
    D. uneducated constituency

24. After an education program has been delivered, an agency conducts a program evaluation to determine whether its objectives have been met. General rules about how to conduct such an education program evaluation include each of the following, EXCEPT that it

   A. must be done immediately after the program has been implemented
   B. should be simple and easy to use
   C. should be designed so that tabulation of responses can take place quickly and inexpensively
   D. should solicit mostly subjective, open-ended responses if the audience was large

25. Using electronic media such as television as means of educating the public is typically recommended ONLY for agencies that
   I. have a fairly simple message to begin with
   II. want to reach the masses, rather than a targeted audience
   III. have substantial financial resources
   IV. accept that they will not be able to measure the results of the campaign with much precision

   A. I and II
   B. I, II and III
   C. II and IV
   D. I, II, III and IV

KEY (CORRECT ANSWERS)

1.	B	11.	C
2.	C	12.	D
3.	D	13.	A
4.	C	14.	D
5.	D	15.	B
6.	B	16.	B
7.	C	17.	D
8.	D	18.	D
9.	D	19.	C
10.	A	20.	D

21.	B
22.	B
23.	C
24.	D
25.	D

EXAMINATION SECTION
TEST 1

DIRECTIONS: Each question or incomplete statement is followed by several suggested answers or completions. Select the one that BEST answers the question or completes the statement. *PRINT THE LETTER OF THE CORRECT ANSWER IN THE SPACE AT THE RIGHT.*

1. A specialist is meeting with a panel of local community leaders to determine their perceptions about the effectiveness of a recent outreach program. The leaders seem unresponsive to the specialist's questions, looking at the floor or each other without directly answering the specialist's questions. One strategy that might work to elicit the desired information would be to

    A. try to discern the hidden meaning of their silence
    B. adopt a mildly confrontational tone and remind them of what's at stake in the community
    C. keep asking open-ended questions and wait patiently for responses
    D. tell them to come back when they're ready to tell you their opinions

    1.____

2. Each of the following statements about maintaining a community's attention is true, EXCEPT

    A. The more challenging it is to pay attention to a message, the more likely it is that it will be attended to.
    B. Listeners will be more motivated to pay attention if a speech is personally meaningful.
    C. People will be more likely to attend if a speaker pauses to suggest natural transitions in a speech.
    D. Listeners will attend to messages that stand out.

    2.____

3. Each of the following is a key strategy to integrative bargaining among community members in conflict, EXCEPT

    A. focusing on positions, rather than interests
    B. separating the people from the problem
    C. aiming for an outcome based on an objectively identified standard
    D. using active listening skills, such as rephrasing and questioning

    3.____

4. Which of the following is NOT one of the major variables to take into account when considering a community needs assessment?

    A. State of program development
    B. Resources available
    C. Demographics
    D. Community attitudes

    4.____

5. Which of the following groups would probably be formed specifically for, or be involved in, the purpose of addressing a specific unmet community need?

    A. An existing consumer group
    B. A council of community representatives
    C. A committee
    D. An existing community organization

    5.____

6. If a public outreach campaign designed to mobilize a community fails, the most likely reason for this failure is that the campaign

   A. was not specific about what they want people to do
   B. are overly serious and do not appeal to people's sense of humor
   C. offered no incentive for the audience to make a change
   D. did not use language that appealed to the audience's emotions

7. Nationwide, the rate of involvement of elderly people in community-based programs demonstrates that they are

   A. underserved when compared to other age groups
   B. served at about the same rate as other age groups
   C. over-served when compared to other age groups
   D. hardly served at all

8. In projecting the likelihood of an education program's success, a domestic violence specialist identifies every single event that must occur to complete the project. The specialist then arranges these events in sequential order and allocates time requirements for each. Finally, the total time is calculated and a model showing all their events and timelines is charted. The specialist has used

   A. a PERT chart
   B. a simulation
   C. a Markov model
   D. the critical path method

9. When working with members of a predominantly African-American community, specialists from other cultural backgrounds should be aware that African Americans tend to express thoughts and feelings through descriptions of

   A. physically tangible sensations
   B. problems to be analyzed
   C. corresponding analogies
   D. spiritual issues

10. Local nonprofessionals should be considered useful to a specialist who is looking to undertake a community outreach or educational initiative. Which of the following is LEAST likely to be a characteristic or role demonstrated by these community members?

    A. Undertaking support functions at the agency
    B. Serving as a communication channel between the agency and clients
    C. Encouraging greater agency acceptance and credibility within the community
    D. Helping the agency to accomplish meaningful change

11. In working with Native American groups or clients, it is important to recognize that the greatest health problem facing their communities today is

    A. domestic violence   B. depression and suicide
    C. alcoholism   D. tuberculosis

12. A specialist is facilitating a cooperative conflict resolution session between community members who have different opinions about what kinds of intervention services should be offered by the local adult protective services agency. Which of the following is NOT a guideline that should be followed in this process?

    A. Early in the negotiations, ask each party to name the issues on which they will positively not yield.
    B. Try to get the parties to view the issue from other points of view, beside the two or three conflicting ones.
    C. Have each side volunteer what it would be willing to do to resolve the conflict.
    D. At the end of the session, draw up a formal agreement with agreed-upon actions for both parties.

13. A specialist wants to evaluate the effectiveness of a local women's shelter. The shelter has suffered from lax participation, given the number of women who have been abused in the surrounding area. The specialist wants to speak with the women in the community who did not follow up on referrals to the shelter, and begins by visiting some of these women. After gaining the trust of these women, the specialist asks for the names of women they know who might be in need of help with a domestic violence situation. The specialist's approach in this case is _____ sampling.

    A. maximum variation   B. snowball
    C. convenience   D. typical case

14. When it comes to perceiving messages, people typically DON'T

    A. tend to simplify causal connections and sometimes even seek a single cause to explain what may be a highly complex effect
    B. tend to perceive messages independently of a categorical framework, especially if the message may be distorted by such an interpretation
    C. have a predisposition toward accepting any pattern that a speaker offers to explain seemingly unconnected facts
    D. tend to interpret things in the way they are viewed by their reference group

15. The elder members of Native American communities, regardless of kinship, are most commonly referred to as

    A. the ancients   B. father or mother
    C. grandfather or grandmother   D. chiefs

16. Each of the following is typically an objective of community mobilization, EXCEPT

    A. To convince existing community resources to alter their services or work together to address an unmet need
    B. To gather and distribute information to consumers and agencies about unmet needs
    C. To publicize existing community resources and make them more accessible
    D. To bring an unmet community need to public attention in order to achieve acceptance of and support for fulfilling the need

17. Research in community outreach shows that women often build friendships through shared positive feelings, whereas men often build friendships through

    A. metacommunication
    B. catharsis
    C. impression management
    D. shared activities

18. Typically, the FIRST step in a community needs assessment is to

    A. identify community's strengths
    B. explore the nature of the neighborhood
    C. get to know the area and its residents
    D. talk to people in the community

19. Most public relations experts agree that _____ exposure(s) to a message is the minimum just to get the message noticed. If the aim of a public outreach campaign is action or a change in behavior, the agency budget must plan for more exposures.

    A. one   B. two   C. three   D. four

20. In the program development/community liaison model of community work and public outreach, the primary constituency is considered to be

    A. community representatives and the service agency board or administrators
    B. elected officials, social agencies, and interagency organizations
    C. marginalized or oppressed population groups in a city or region
    D. residents of a neighborhood, parish or rural county

21. Social or interpersonal problems in many African American communities have their roots in

    A. personality deficits
    B. unresolved family conflicts
    C. poor communication
    D. external stressors

22. A public outreach campaign should
    I. focus on short-term, measurable goals, rather than ultimate outcomes
    II. try to alter entrenched attitudes within a short time, with powerfully worded messages
    III. proceed in steps or phases, each of which lays out a mechanism that leads to the desired effect
    IV. ignore causes that led to a problem, and instead focus on solutions

    A. I and II   B. II and III   C. III only   D. I, II, III and IV

23. Research findings indicate that in listing preferences for helping professional attributes, individuals from culturally diverse groups are MOST likely to_____ as more important than

    A. personality similarity; either race/ethnic similarity or attitude similarity
    B. therapist experience; any kind of similarity
    C. race/ethnic similarity; attitude similarity
    D. attitude similarity; race/ethnic similarity

24. Each of the following is considered to be an objective of community organization, EXCEPT
    A. effecting changes in the distribution of decision-making power
    B. helping people develop and strengthen the traits of self-direction and cooperation
    C. effecting and maintaining the balance between needs and resources in a community
    D. helping people deal with their problems by developing alternative behaviors

25. A specialist is helping the adult protective services agency to design a public outreach campaign. The topic to be addressed is complex, public understanding is low, and most professionals at the agency feel that having more complete information might change the opinions of community members. Which method of pre-campaign research is probably most appropriate?
    A. Deliberative polling
    B. Attitude scales
    C. Surveys or questionnaires
    D. Focus groups

KEY (CORRECT ANSWERS)

1. C		11. C	
2. A		12. A	
3. A		13. B	
4. C		14. B	
5. C		15. C	
6. A		16. B	
7. A		17. D	
8. D		18. B	
9. C		19. C	
10. A		20. A	

21. D
22. C
23. D
24. D
25. A

TEST 2

DIRECTIONS: Each question or incomplete statement is followed by several suggested answers or completions. Select the one the BEST answers the question or completes the statement. *PRINT THE LETTER OF THE CORRECT ANSWER IN THE SPACE AT THE RIGHT.*

1. A specialist has been called in to resolve a dispute between two community leaders who have been arguing about the level of service needed within the community. The discussion has been going on for several hours when the specialist arrives, and both people seem to be upset. After calming the two down and getting each of them to agree on a statement of the problem, the specialist should ask each person to

    A. summarize his or her argument in three main points
    B. explain why he or she became so upset
    C. clearly state, in objective terms, the position of the other in a form that meets with the other's approval
    D. identify the best alternative outcome, other than their presumed ideal

    1.____

2. In evaluation the impact of a public outreach campaign, the _____ model can be used early in he campaign to address first impressions.

    A. exposure or advertising
    B. expert interview
    C. impact monitoring or process
    D. experimental or quasi-experimental

    2.____

3. When trying to motivate an older population to take action on a community problem, it is helpful to remember that older people

    A. are more self-reliant in their decision-making than other members of the same family
    B. often need more time to decide than younger people
    C. are more likely than younger people to view community problems self-referentially
    D. tend to take a pragmatic, rather than philosophical, view of life

    3.____

4. The method of group or community decision-making that is normally most time-consuming is

    A. majority opinion
    B. consensus
    C. expert opinion
    D. authority rule

    4.____

5. A local adult protective services agency has identified one of the goals of its recent public outreach campaign to be the mobilization of activists. The campaign should probably

    A. target neutral audiences
    B. home in on supporters
    C. stick to purely factual information
    D. try to persuade community fence-sitters

    5.____

6. Research of Native American youths' perceptions of family concerns for their well-being has generally found that these youths

   A. have a high degree of uncertainty about their families' feelings toward them
   B. believe their families don't care about them
   C. believe that their mothers care a great deal about them, but their fathers don't
   D. believe their families care a great deal about them

7. A domestic violence specialist is developing a new outreach program for the local community. The specialist has defined the target problem, set program goals, and planned the actions that will take place as a result of the program. Most likely, the next step will be to

   A. evaluate the resources available to achieve program goals
   B. define and sequence the steps that will be taken to achieve program goals
   C. determine how the program will be evaluated
   D. decide how the program will operate

8. In the following exchange, what listening skill is evident in the underlined statement?

   Elder: *I'm so glad to have someone to talk to, someone who really understands my problem.*
   Specialist: *It is nice to be able to talk to someone who will listen.*
   Elder: That's for sure.

   A. verbatim response
   B. paraphrasing
   C. advising
   D. evaluation

9. Which of the following activities is involved in the specialist's task of mobilizing?

   A. Meeting individuals in the community with problems and assisting them in finding help
   B. Identifying unmet community needs
   C. Speaking out against an unjust policy or procedure
   D. Developing new services or linking presently available services to meet community needs

10. The preliminary research associated with a public outreach campaign should FIRST be aimed at determining

    A. the budget
    B. the message's ultimate audience
    C. what media to use
    D. the short-term behavioral goals of the campaign

11. A specialist in a low-income community wants to plan programs that will deal with the influence of unemployment on domestic disturbances. The specialist needs to know not only how many unemployed people are in the community now, but also how many people will be unemployed at any particular time in the future, and how those numbers will vary given certain conditions. Probably the best way to trace employment rates over time and within differing conditions is through the use of

A. the critical path method   B. linear programming
C. difference equations   D. the Markov model

12. Generally, public outreach programs—whatever their stated goal—should
    I. create a sense of urgency about a problem
    II. decline to identify opponents of the issue or idea
    III. propose concrete, easily understandable solutions
    IV. urge a specific action

    A. I only   B. I, III and IV   C. II and III   D. I, II, III and IV

13. Which of the following methods of community needs assessment relies to the greatest degree on existing public records?

    A. Social indicators   B. Field study
    C. Rates-under treatment   D. Key informant

14. During an interview with a Native American client, a specialist is careful to maintain close and nearly constant eye contact. The client is most likely to interpret this as

    A. a show of high concern
    B. a sign of disrespect
    C. an uncomfortable assumption of intimacy
    D. an attempt to intimidate

15. The best strategy for addressing an audience that is known to be captive, or even hostile, is to

    A. refer to experiences in common
    B. flatter the audience
    C. joke about things in or near the audience
    D. plead for fairness

16. Integrative conflict resolution is characterized by

    A. an overriding concern to maximize joint outcomes
    B. one side's interests opposing the other's
    C. a fixed and limited amount of resources to be divided, so that the more one group gets, the less another gets
    D. manipulation and withholding information as negotiation strategies

17. A specialist wants to learn how to interact with the members of a largely Latino community in a more culturally sensitive way. Which of the following is NOT a guideline for interacting with members of a Latino community?

    A. Efforts to foster independence and self-reliance may be interpreted by many Latinos as a lack of concern for others.
    B. Efforts to deal one-on-one with an adolescent client may serve to alienate the parents, especially the mother.
    C. A nonverbal gesture such as lowering the eyes is interpreted by many Latinos as a sign of respect and deference to authority.
    D. In much of Latino culture, the locus of control for problems tends to be much more external than internal.

18. Each of the following is an supporting assumption of community organization, EXCEPT   18.____

    A. democracy requires cooperative participation
    B. in order for communities to change, it is necessary for each individual in the community to be willing to change
    C. communities often need help with organization and planning
    D. holistic approaches work better than fragmented or ad-hoc programs

19. Helping professionals often have difficulty to bring community resources together to fulfill unmet community needs. Which of the following is NOT usually a reason for this?   19.____

    A. Some community groups resist assistance when it is offered.
    B. Few community groups make their needs known.
    C. Community resources frequently change the type of services they offer.
    D. Often, community resources prefer to work alone

20. When dealing with groups or populations of elderly clients, specialists should be mindful that about _____ of the nation's elderly suffer from mental health problems.   20.____

    A. a tenth   B. a quarter   C. a third   D. half

21. In an African American community, a specialist from another culture should recognize that church participation, for most African Americans, is viewed as a   21.____

    A. method for maintaining control and communicating competency
    B. way of depersonalizing problems or troubles
    C. way to divert attention away from problems
    D. means of cathartic emotional release

22. Adult protective service programs supported by state statutes protect elderly people from abuse and neglect under the doctrine of   22.____

    A. parens patriae   B. habeas corpus
    C. in loco parentis   D. volenti non fit injuria

23. In terms of public outreach, which of the following statements about an audience is NOT generally true?   23.____

    A. The more heterogeneous the audience, the more necessary it will be to use specific examples and appeals to certain types of people
    B. The smaller the audience, the more likely that its members will share assumptions and values
    C. When the speaker does not know the status of an audience, it is best to assume that they are captive rather than voluntary
    D. The larger an audience, the more formal a presentation is likely to be

24. A specialist often spends time in the places frequented by community residents. She listens carefully to what residents seem most concerned about, and engages many in conversations, asking them how they see the problems in the community. During these conversations, she makes mental notes about whether the statements of the problems are the same things that are mentioned in their conversations. From these conversations, the worker determines what she thinks the unmet needs of the community are. Which of the key issues in identifying unmet needs has the worker neglected to address?   24.___

    A. The different points of view regarding the issues, and whether there is any common ground.
    B. Whether the stated problems and the conversations with community residents reflect the same concerns.
    C. How community residents define the issues.
    D. What the residents talk about with one another in a community.

25. Which of the following political styles should be used to promote an issue that could become controversial if it is perceived to involve major reforms?   25.___

    A. High-conflict, polarized
    B. High-conflict, consensual
    C. Moderate conflict, compromise-oriented
    D. Low-conflict, technical

KEY (CORRECT ANSWERS)

1. C
2. A
3. B
4. B
5. B

6. D
7. A
8. B
9. D
10. B

11. D
12. B
13. A
14. B
15. A

16. A
17. D
18. B
19. C
20. B

21. D
22. A
23. A
24. A
25. D

READING COMPREHENSION
UNDERSTANDING AND INTERPRETING WRITTEN MATERIAL
EXAMINATION SECTION
TEST 1

Questions 1-23.

DIRECTIONS: Each question consists of a statement. You are to indicate whether the statement is TRUE (T) or FALSE (F). *PRINT THE LETTER OF THE CORRECT ANSWER IN THE SPACE AT THE RIGHT.*

Questions 1-8.

DIRECTIONS: Questions 1 through 8 are based on the following passage. Read the passage carefully and then answer these questions ONLY on the basis of the information contained in this passage.

Displacement tonnage is the actual weight in tons of 2,240 pounds which a vessel displaces when floating at any given draft. This naturally varies with the draft. The displacement is calculated by figuring the volume of the vessel under water in cubic feet and dividing by 35, since 35 cubic feet of sea water weigh one ton (2,240 pounds). Deadweight tonnage is the carrying capacity of a vessel figured by weight in terms of tons of 2,240 pounds. If her displacement were calculated when the vessel was light and again when she was loaded, the difference would express the deadweight tonnage.

1. In figuring displacement, the short ton (2,000 pounds) is used. 1.____

2. One cubic foot of sea water weighs approximately 35 pounds. 2.____

3. Displacement tonnage varies with the draft. 3.____

4. Displacement tonnage is the weight of the cargo in tons. 4.____

5. The carrying capacity of a vessel is called the deadweight tonnage. 5.____

6. To calculate the deadweight tonnage, subtract the ship's displacement when light from its displacement when fully loaded. 6.____

7. If the volume of a vessel under water is 700 cubic feet, its displacement tonnage is 20 tons. 7.____

8. The vessel is said to be *light* when she does not have her cargo aboard. 8.____

Questions 9-16.

DIRECTIONS: Questions 9 through 16 are based on the following passage. Read the passage carefully and then answer these questions ONLY on the basis of the information contained in this passage.

Boats of Classes 1, 2, and 3 must carry an efficient whistle *or other sound-producing mechanical appliance.* This is used to give both passing signals and fog signals. A fog horn is not required on motor boats and should not be used in place of a whistle. On Class 1, the whistle or sound-producing mechanical appliance (air or electric horn) may be hand, mouth, or power-operated, and must be audible at least ½ mile. On Class 2, it must be hand or power-operated, audible at least 1 mile. On Class 3, it must be power-operated, audible at least 1 mile. In every case, the whistle must be capable of producing a blast of 2 seconds or more duration. The whistle is not required on Class A (less than 16 feet).

9. Only Class 3 boats must have power-operated whistles. 9.___

10. Whistles on Class 1 boats must be audible for a greater distance than whistles on Class 2 boats. 10.___

11. On motorboats, a fog horn may be used in place of a whistle 11.___

12. Boats of all classes are required to carry a whistle. 12.___

13. The whistle on boats of Classes 1, 2, and 3 may be used to give fog signals. 13.___

14. The whistle on boats of Classes 1, 2, and 3 must be able to produce a blast of more than 3 seconds. 14.___

15. Boats of Class A are less than 16 feet long. 15.___

16. In place of a whistle, any similar sound-producing mechanical appliance may be used on boats of Classes 1, 2, and 3. 16.___

Questions 17-23.

DIRECTIONS: Questions 17 through 23 are based on the following paragraph. Read the paragraph and then answer the questions.

At about 12 noon aboard the sludge boat LIBERTY, we are well into the Ambrose Channel. The fog shuts in so thickly that we can scarcely see. We become concerned for we are in the busiest marine highway in the world, through which all of the biggest vessels afloat may and do pass day after day. We must stay on our right side of the channel, and look sharply for all *black* buoys. If only all ships coming in the opposite direction will stay on their right side or the channel and look just as sharply for their *red* buoys, then we will be safe. Our automatic fog whistle drones away, at regular intervals. Our courage is fortified by the knowledge that the men on our ships have traveled this highway scores of times and are thoroughly familiar with its landmarks. The fog becomes so thick the captain stops his vessel. Hearing no danger signals ahead and sure of his position on the right side of the channel, along the black buoys, he moves ahead slowly—then stops—then crawls ahead again. It is a time of tension – of uneasiness – for anything might happen. It is a few minutes past noon. The entire watch is vigilant. Look-outs are up in the eyes of the ship. Suddenly the look-out reports a great hulk of an oncoming vessel bearing down upon us. Our captain rings his engines *full speed astern* as he blows to tell the other vessel of his maneuver. Our captain blows the dannger signal. The other vessel does the same but it is too late. She crashes into our port side with a force that might well drive us to the bottom. She is the Texas Oil tanker FARMER, with a full load of high test gasoline. A single spark—gasoline! The collision of two steel vessels could supply these sparks. Fortunately, the calamity does not become a catastrophe. Our vessel stays afloat. It is not necessary to take to the boats. We anchor until the fog lifts.

17. The LIBERTY was proceeding from seaward. 17._____

18. The automatic fog whistle was sounding at intervals of not more than one minute apart. 18._____

19. Each blast of the fog whistle should have been of at least 12 seconds duration 19._____

20. The captain of the LIBERTY should not have stopped the vessel in the thick fog. 20._____

21. When the captain of the LIBERTY informed the other vessel that the engines were full speed astern, he did so by giving three short blasts. 21._____

22. The danger signal given by each vessel consisted of at least four short blasts 22._____

23. Following the crash, while the LIBERTY was at anchor, the rules of the road did not apply to her. 23._____

Questions 24-30.

DIRECTIONS: Each question or incomplete statement is followed by several suggested answers or completions. Select the one that BEST answers the question or completes the statement. *PRINT THE LETTER OF THE CORRECT ANSWER IN THE SPACE AT THE RIGHT.*

Questions 24-26.

DIRECTIONS: Questions 24 through 26 are to be answered in accordance with the information given in the following paragraph.

Tides are the periodic rise and fall of ocean waters, occurring about twice a day, becoming later each day,... due to the gravitational pull of the moon and to a smaller extent the sun...The tides rise highest when the sun and moon are on the same side of the earth (Spring tides), and are lowest (Neap tides) when the sun and moon are in opposition. Local tides depend on irregularities in the floor and coast of the ocean.

24. According to the above paragraph, if high tide is at 7 A.M. on a certain day, the next day's high tide FIRST occurs 24._____

   A. slightly earlier than 7 A.M.
   B. slightly later than 7 A.M.
   C. at exactly 7 A.M.
   D. at exactly 7 P.M.

25. According to the above paragraph, the HIGHEST tides are called _____ tides. 25._____

   A. Spring   B. Summer   C. Fall   D. Winter

26. According to the above paragraph, the Neap tides occur when the 26._____

   A. moon is in its third quarter
   B. moon and sun are on the same side of the earth
   C. sun and moon are in opposition
   D. moon is in its first quarter

Questions 27-30.

DIRECTIONS: Questions 27 through 30 are to be answered ONLY on the basis of the information given in the following paragraph.

The National and city flags are displayed daily from those public buildings which are equipped with vertical or horizontal flag staffs. Where a building has only one flag staff, only the National flag is displayed. When the National flag is to be raised at the same time as other flags, the National flag shall be raised about 6 feet in advance of the other flags; if the flags are raised separately, the National flag shall always be raised first. When more than one flag is flown on horizontal staffs, the National flag shall be flown so that it is to the extreme left as the observer faces the flag. When more than one flag is displayed, they should all be the same size. Under no circumstances should the National flag be smaller in size than any other flag in a combination display. The standard size for flags flown from city buildings is 5' x 8'.

27. From the above paragraph, a reasonable conclusion about flag staffs on public buildings is that a public building

   A. might have no flag staff at all
   B. needs two flag staffs
   C. should have at least one flag staff
   D. usually has a horizontal and a vertical flag staff

28. According to the above paragraph, a public building that has only one flag staff should raise the National flag

   A. and no other flag
   B. at sunrise
   C. first and then the city flag
   D. six feet in advance of any other flag

29. According to the above paragraph, the order, from left to right, in which the National flag flying from one of four horizontal staffs should appear to a person who is facing the flag staffs is

   A. flag 1, flag 2, flag 3, National flag
   B. National flag, flag 1, flag 2, flag 3
   C. flag 1, flag 2, National flag, flag 3
   D. flag 1, National flag, flag 2, flag 3

30. According to the above paragraph, a combination display of flags on a city building would USUALLY have

   A. a 6'x10' National flag
   B. all flags of 5' x 8' size
   C. all other flags smaller than the National flag
   D. 5' x 8' National and city flags and smaller sized other flags

KEY (CORRECT ANSWERS)

1.	F	16.	T
2.	F	17.	F
3.	T	18.	T
4.	F	19.	F
5.	T	20.	F
6.	T	21.	T
7.	T	22.	T
8.	T	23.	T
9.	T	24.	B
10.	F	25.	A
11.	F	26.	C
12.	F	27.	A
13.	T	28.	A
14.	F	29.	B
15.	T	30.	B

READING COMPREHENSION
UNDERSTANDING AND INTERPRETING WRITTEN MATERIAL
EXAMINATION SECTION
TEST 1

DIRECTIONS: Each question or incomplete statement is followed by several suggested answers or completions. Select the one that BEST answers the question or completes the statement. *PRINT THE LETTER OF THE CORRECT ANSWER IN THE SPACE AT THE RIGHT.*

Questions 1-3.

DIRECTIONS: Questions 1 through 3 are to be answered SOLELY on the basis of the following passage.

When police officers search for a stolen car, they first check for the color of the car, then for make, model, year, body damage, and finally license number. The first five can be detected from almost any angle, while the recognition of the license number is often not immediately apparent. The serial number and motor number, though less likely to be changed than the easily substituted license number, cannot be observed in initial detection of the stolen car.

1. According to the above passage, the one of the following features which is LEAST readily observed in checking for a stolen car in moving traffic is

    A. license number   B. serial number   C. model
    D. make   E. color

1.____

2. The feature of a car that cannot be determined from most angles of observation is the

    A. make   B. model   C. year
    D. license number   E. color

2.____

3. Of the following, the feature of a stolen car that is MOST likely to be altered by a car thief shortly after the car is stolen is the

    A. license number   B. motor number   C. color
    D. model   E. minor body damage

3.____

Questions 4-5.

DIRECTIONS: Questions 4 and 5 are to be answered SOLELY on the basis of the following passage.

The racketeer is primarily concerned with business affairs, legitimate or otherwise, and preferably those which are close to the margin of legitimacy. He gets his best opportunities from business organizations which meet the need of large sections of the public for goods or services which are defined as illegitimate by the same public, such as prostitution, gambling, illicit drugs or liquor. In contrast to the thief, the racketeer and the establishments he controls deliver goods and services for money received.

4. From the above passage, it can be deduced that suppression of racketeers is difficult because

   A. victims of racketeers are not guilty of violating the law
   B. racketeers are generally engaged in fully legitimate enterprises
   C. many people want services which are not obtainable through legitimate sources
   D. the racketeers are well organized
   E. laws prohibiting gambling and prostitution are unenforceable

4.____

5. According to the above passage, racketeering, unlike theft, involves

   A. objects of value
   B. payment for goods received
   C. organized gangs
   D. public approval
   E. unlawful activities

5.____

Questions 6-8.

DIRECTIONS: Questions 6 through 8 are to be answered SOLELY on the basis of the following passage.

A number of crimes, such as robbery, assault, rape, certain forms of theft and burglary, are high visibility crimes in that it is apparent to all concerned that they are criminal acts prior to or at the time they are committed. In contrast to these, check forgeries, especially those committed by first offenders, have low visibility. There is little in the criminal act or in the interaction between the check passer and the person cashing the check to identify it as a crime. Closely related to this special quality of the forgery crime is the fact that, while it is formally defined and treated as a felonious or infamous crime, it is informally held by the legally untrained public to be a relatively harmless form of crime.

6. According to the above passage, crimes of *high visibility*

   A. are immediately recognized as crimes by the victims
   B. take place in public view
   C. always involve violence or the threat of violence
   D. usually are committed after dark
   E. can be observed from a distance

6.____

7. According to the above passage,

   A. the public regards check forgery as a minor crime
   B. the law regards check forgery as a minor crime
   C. the law distinguishes between check forgery and other forgery
   D. it is easier to spot inexperienced check forgers than other criminals
   E. it is more difficult to identify check forgers than other criminals

7.____

8. As used in the above passage, an *infamous* crime is

   A. a crime attracting great attention from the public
   B. more serious than a felony
   C. less serious than a felony

8.____

D. more or less serious than a felony depending upon the surrounding circumstances
E. the same as a felony

Questions 9-11.

DIRECTIONS: Questions 9 through 11 are to be answered SOLELY on the basis of the following passage.

Criminal science is largely the science of identification. Progress in this field has been marked and sometimes very spectacular because new techniques, instruments, and facts flow continuously from the scientists. But the crime laboratories are undermanned, trade secrets still prevail, and inaccurate conclusions are often the result. However, modern gadgets cannot substitute for the skilled intelligent investigator; he must be their master.

9. According to the above passage, criminal science   9._____

   A. excludes the field of investigation
   B. is primarily interested in establishing identity
   C. is based on the equipment used in crime laboratories
   D. uses techniques different from those used in other sciences
   E. is essentially secret in nature

10. Advances in criminal science have been, according to the above passage,   10._____

    A. extremely limited   B. slow but steady
    C. unusually reliable   D. outstanding
    E. infrequently worthwhile

11. A problem that has NOT been overcome completely in crime work is, according to the   11._____
    above passage,

    A. unskilled investigators
    B. the expense of new equipment and techniques
    C. an insufficient number of personnel in crime laboratories
    D. inaccurate equipment used in laboratories
    E. conclusions of the public about the value of this field

Questions 12-14.

DIRECTIONS: Questions 12 through 14 are to be answered SOLELY on the basis of the following passage.

The New York City Police Department will accept for investigation no report of a person missing from his residence, if such residence is located outside of New York City. The person reporting same will be advised to report such fact to the police department of the locality where the missing person lives, which will, if necessary, communicate officially with the New York City Police Department. However, a report will be accepted of a person who is missing from a temporary residence in New York City, but the person making the report will be instructed to make a report also to the police department of the locality where the missing person lives.

12. According to the above passage, a report to the New York City Police Department of a missing person whose permanent residence is outside of New York City will   12.____

    A. always be investigated provided that a report is also made to his local police authorities
    B. never be investigated unless requested officially by his local police authorities
    C. be investigated in cases of temporary New York City residence, but a report should always be made to his local police authorities
    D. be investigated if the person making the report is a New York City resident
    E. always be investigated and a report will be made to the local police authorities by the New York City Police Department

13. Of the following, the MOST likely reason for the procedure described in the above paragraph is that   13.____

    A. non-residents are not entitled to free police service from New York City
    B. local police authorities would resent interference in their jurisdiction
    C. local police authorities sometimes try to unload their problems on the New York City Police
    D. local police authorities may be better able to conduct an investigation
    E. few persons are erroneously reported as missing

14. Mr. Smith, who lives in Jersey City, and Mr. Jones, who lives in Newark arrange to meet in New York City, but Mr. Jones doesn't keep the appointment. Mr. Smith telephones Mr. Jones several times the next day and gets no answer. Mr. Smith believes that something has happened to Mr. Jones.   14.____
    According to the above passage, Mr. Smith should apply to the police authorities of

    A. Jersey City
    B. Newark
    C. Newark and New York City
    D. Jersey City and New York City
    E. Newark, Jersey City, and New York City

Questions 15-17.

DIRECTIONS: Questions 15 through 17 are to be answered SOLELY on the basis of the following passage.

Some early psychologists believed that the basic characteristic of the criminal type was inferiority of intelligence, if not outright feeblemindedness. They were misled by the fact that they had measurements for all kinds of criminals, but, until World War I gave them a draft army sample, they had no information on a comparable group of non-criminal adults. As soon as acceptable measurements could be taken of criminals and a comparable group of non-criminals, concern with feeblemindedness or with low intelligence as a type took on less and less significance in research in criminology.

15. According to the above passage, some early psychologists were in error because they didn't   15.____

    A. distinguish among the various types of criminals
    B. devise a suitable method of measuring intelligence

C. measure the intelligence of non-criminals as a basis for comparison
D. distinguish between feeblemindedness and inferiority of intelligence
E. clearly define the term *intelligence*

16. The above passage implies that studies of the intelligence of criminals and non-criminals 16._____

    A. are useless because it is impossible to obtain comparable groups
    B. are not meaningful because only the less intelligent criminals are detected
    C. indicate that criminals are more intelligent than non-criminals
    D. indicate that criminals are less intelligent than non-criminals
    E. do not indicate that there are any differences between the two groups

17. According to the above passage, studies of the World War I draft gave psychologists vital 17._____
    information concerning

    A. adaptability to army life of criminals and non-criminals
    B. criminal tendencies among draftees
    C. the intelligence scores of large numbers of men
    D. differences between intelligence scores of draftees and volunteers
    E. the behavior of men under abnormal conditions

Questions 18-20.

DIRECTIONS: Questions 18 through 20 are to be answered SOLELY on the basis of the following passage.

The use of a roadblock is simply an adaptation to police practices of the military concept of encirclement. Successful operation of a roadblock plan depends almost entirely on the amount of advance study and planning given to such operations. A thorough and detailed examination of the roads and terrain under the jurisdiction of a given police agency should be made with the locations of the roadblocks pinpointed in advance. The first principle to be borne in mind in the location of each roadblock is the time element. Its location must be at a point beyond which the fugitive could not have possibly traveled in the time elapsed from the commission of the crime to the arrival of the officers at the roadblock.

18. According to the above passage, 18._____

    A. military operations have made extensive use of road-blocks
    B. the military concept of encirclement is an adaptation of police use of roadblocks
    C. the technique of encirclement has been widely used by military forces
    D. a roadblock is generally more effective than encirclement
    E. police use of roadblocks is based on the idea of military encirclement

19. According to the above passage, 19._____

    A. the factor of time is the sole consideration in the location of a roadblock
    B. the maximum speed possible in the method of escape is of major importance in roadblock location
    C. the time of arrival of officers at the site of a proposed roadblock is of little importance

D. if the method of escape is not known, it should be assumed that the escape is by automobile
E. a roadblock should be sited as close to the scene of the crime as the terrain will permit

20. According to the above passage, 20.___

   A. advance study and planning are of minor importance in the success of roadblock operations
   B. a thorough and detailed examination of all roads within a radius of fifty miles should precede the determination of a roadblock location
   C. consideration of terrain features are important in planning the location of road-blocks
   D. the pinpointing of roadblocks should be performed before any advance study is made
   E. a roadblock operation can seldom be successfully undertaken by a single police agency

---

KEY (CORRECT ANSWERS)

1. B	6. A	11. C	16. E
2. D	7. A	12. C	17. C
3. A	8. E	13. D	18. E
4. C	9. B	14. B	19. B
5. B	10. D	15. C	20. C

TEST 2

DIRECTIONS: Each question or incomplete statement is followed by several suggested answers or completions. Select the one that BEST answers the question or completes the statement. *PRINT THE LETTER OF THE CORRECT ANSWER IN THE SPACE AT THE RIGHT.*

Questions 1-3.

DIRECTIONS: Questions 1 through 3 are to be answered SOLELY on the basis of the following passage.

Modern police science may be said to have three phases. The first phase embraces the identification of living and dead persons. The second embraces the field work carried out by specially trained detectives at the scene of the crime. The third embraces methods used in the police laboratory to examine and analyze clues and traces discovered in the course of the investigation. While modern police science has had a striking influence on detective work and will surely further enhance its effectiveness, the time-honored methods and practical detective work will always be important. The time-honored methods, that is, knowledge of methods used by criminals, patience, tact, industry, thoroughness, and imagination, will always be requisites for successful detective work.

1. According to the above passage, we may expect modern police science to   1.____

    A. help detective work more and more
    B. become more and more scientific
    C. depend less and less on the time-honored methods
    D. bring together the many different approaches to detective work
    E. play a less important role in detective work

2. According to the above passage, a knowledge of the procedures used by criminals is   2.____

    A. solely an element of the modern police science approach to detective work
    B. related to the identification of persons
    C. not related to detective field work
    D. related to methods used in the police laboratory
    E. an element of the traditional approach to detective work

3. Modern police science and practical detective work, according to the above passage,   3.____

    A. when used together can only lead to confusion
    B. are based on distinctly different theories of detective work
    C. have had strikingly different influences on detective work
    D. should both be used for successful detective work
    E. lead usually to similar results

Questions 4-7.

DIRECTIONS: Questions 4 through 7 are to be answered SOLELY on the basis of the following passage.

A member of the force shall render reasonable aid to a sick or injured person. He shall summon an ambulance, if necessary, by-telephoning the communications bureau of the borough, who shall notify the precinct concerned. If possible, he shall wait in full view of the arriving ambulance and take necessary action to direct the responding doctor or attendant to the patient, without delay. If the ambulance does not arrive in twenty minutes, he shall send in a second call. However, if the sick person is in his or her own home, a member of the force, before summoning an ambulance, will ascertain whether such person is willing to be taken to a hospital for treatment.

4. According to the above passage, if a patrolman wants to get an ambulance for a sick person, he should telephone

    A. the precinct concerned
    B. only if the sick person is in his home
    C. the nearest hospital
    D. only if the sick person is not in his home
    E. the borough communications bureau

5. According to the above passage, if a patrolman telephones for an ambulance and none arrives within twenty minutes, he should

    A. ask the injured person if he is willing to be taken to a hospital
    B. call the borough communications bureau
    C. call the precinct concerned
    D. attempt to give the injured person such assistance as he may need
    E. call the nearest hospital

6. A patrolman is called to help a woman who has fallen in her own home and has apparently broken her leg. According to the above passage, he should

    A. ask her if she wants to go to a hospital
    B. try to set her leg if it is necessary
    C. call for an ambulance at once
    D. attempt to get a doctor as quickly as possible
    E. not attempt to help the woman in any way before competent medical aid arrives

7. A man falls from a window into the backyard of an apartment house. Assume that you are a patrolman and that you are called to assist this man.
   According to the above passage, after you have called for an ambulance and comforted the injured man as much as you can, you should

    A. wait in front of the house for the ambulance
    B. ask the injured man if he wishes to go to the hospital for treatment
    C. remain with the injured man until the ambulance arrives
    D. send a bystander to direct the nearest doctor to the patient
    E. not ask the man to explain how the accident happened

Questions 8-10.

DIRECTIONS: Questions 8 through 10 are to be answered SOLELY on the basis of the following passage.

What is required is a program that will protect our citizens and their property from criminal and antisocial acts, will effectively restrain and reform juvenile delinquents, and will prevent the further development of antisocial behavior. Discipline and punishment of offenders must necessarily play an important part in any such program. Serious offenders cannot be mollycoddled merely because they are under twenty-one. Restraint and punishment necessarily follow serious antisocial acts. But punishment, if it is to be effective, must be a planned part of a more comprehensive program of treating delinquency.

8. The one of the following goals NOT included among those listed above is to 8.____

   A. stop young people from defacing public property
   B. keep homes from being broken into
   C. develop an intra-city boys' baseball league
   D. change juvenile delinquents into useful citizens
   E. prevent young people from developing antisocial behavior patterns

9. According to the above passage, punishment is 9.____

   A. not satisfactory in any program dealing with juvenile delinquents
   B. the most effective means by which young vandals and hooligans can be reformed
   C. not used sufficiently when dealing with serious offenders who are under twenty-one
   D. of value in reducing juvenile delinquency only if it is part of a complete program
   E. most effective when it does not relate to specific antisocial acts

10. With respect to serious offenders who are under twenty-one, the above passage suggests that they 10.____

    A. be mollycoddled
    B. be dealt with as part of a comprehensive program to punish mature criminals
    C. should be punished
    D. be prevented, by brute force if necessary, from performing antisocial acts
    E. be treated as delinquent children who require more love than punishment

Questions 11-14.

DIRECTIONS: Questions 11 through 14 are to be answered SOLELY on the basis of the following passage.

In all cases of homicide, members of the Police Department who investigate will make every effort to obtain statements from dying persons. Such statements are of the greatest importance to the District Attorney. In many cases, there may be a failure to solve the crime if they are not taken. The principal element to be considered in taking the declaration of a dying person is his mental attitude. In order to be admissible in evidence, the person must have no hope of recovery. The patient will be fully interrogated on that point before a statement is taken.

11. In cases of homicide, according to the above passage, members of the police force will

    A. try to change the mental attitude of the dying person
    B. attempt to obtain a statement from the dying person
    C. not give the information they obtain directly to the District Attorney
    D. be careful not to injure the dying person unnecessarily
    E. prevent unauthorized persons from taking dying declarations

12. The mental attitude of the person making the dying statement is of great importance because it can determine, according to the above passage, whether the

    A. victim should be interrogated in the presence of witnesses
    B. victim will be willing to make a statement of any kind
    C. victim has been forced to make the statement
    D. statement will tell the District Attorney who committed the crime
    E. statement can be used as evidence

13. District Attorneys find that statements of a dying person are important, according to the above paragraph, because

    A. it may be that the victim will recover and refuse to testify
    B. they are important elements in determining the mental attitude of the victim
    C. they present a point of view
    D. it may be impossible to punish the criminal without such a statement
    E. dead men tell no tales

14. A well-known gangster is found dying from a bullet wound. The patrolman first on the scene, in the presence of witnesses, tells the man that he is going to die and asks, *Who shot you?* The gangster says, *Jones shot me, but he hasn't killed me. I'll live to get him.* He then falls back dead.
    According to the above passage, this statement is

    A. admissible in evidence; the man was obviously speaking the truth
    B. not admissible in evidence; the man obviously did not believe that he was dying
    C. admissible in evidence; there were witnesses to the statement
    D. not admissible in evidence; the victim did not sign any statement and the evidence is merely hearsay
    E. admissible in evidence; there was no time to interrogate the victim

Questions 15-17.

DIRECTIONS: Questions 15 through 17 are to be answered SOLELY on the basis of the following passage.

The factors contributing to crime and delinquency are varied and complex. The home and its immediate environment have been found to be crucial in determining the behavior patterns of the individual, and criminality can frequently be traced to faulty family relationships and a bad neighborhood. But in the search for a clearer understanding of the underlying causes of delinquent and criminal behavior, the total environment must be taken into consideration.

15. According to the above passage, family relationships

    A. tend to become faulty in bad neighborhoods
    B. are important in determining the actions of honest people as well as Criminals
    C. are the only important element in the understanding of causes of delinquency
    D. are determined by the total environment
    E. of criminals are understandable only in terms of the behavior patterns of the individuals concerned

16. According to the above passage, the causes of crime and delinquency are

    A. not simple
    B. not meaningless
    C. meaningless
    D. simple
    E. always understandable

17. According to the above passage, faulty family relationships frequently are

    A. responsible for varied and complex results
    B. caused by differences
    C. caused when one or both parents have a criminal behavior pattern
    D. independent of the total environment
    E. the cause of criminal acts

Questions 18-20.

DIRECTIONS: Questions 18 through 20 are to be answered SOLELY on the basis of the following passage.

A change in the specific problems which confront the police and in the methods for dealing with them has taken place in the last few decades. The automobile is a two-way symbol of this change in policing. It menaces every city with a complicated traffic problem and has speeded up the process of committing a crime and making a getaway, but at the same time has increased the effectiveness of police operations. However, the major concern of police departments continues to be the antisocial or criminal actions and behavior of human beings.

18. On the basis of the above passage, it can be stated that for the most part in the past few decades, the specific problems of a police force

    A. have changed but the general problems have not
    B. as well as the general problems have changed
    C. have remained the same but the general problems have changed
    D. as well as the general problems have remained the same
    E. have caused changes in the general problems

19. According to the above passage, advances in science and industry have, in general, made the police

    A. operations less effective from the overall point of view
    B. operations more effective from the overall point of view
    C. abandon older methods of solving police problems
    D. concern themselves more with the antisocial acts of human beings
    E. concern themselves less with the antisocial acts of human beings

20. The automobile is *a two-way symbol,* according to the above passage, because its use   20.___
    A. has speeded up getting to, and away from, the scene of a crime
    B. both helps and hurts police operations
    C. introduces a new antisocial act—traffic violation—and does away with criminals like horse thieves
    D. both increases and decreases speed by introducing traffic problems
    E. helps people get to the city but prevents them from moving once they are there

---

KEY (CORRECT ANSWERS)

1. A	6. A	11. B	16. A
2. E	7. A	12. E	17. E
3. D	8. C	13. D	18. A
4. E	9. D	14. B	19. B
5. B	10. C	15. B	20. B

PREPARING WRITTEN MATERIAL

EXAMINATION SECTION
TEST 1

DIRECTIONS: Each question or incomplete statement is followed by several suggested answers or completions. Select the one that BEST answers the question or completes the statement. *PRINT THE LETTER OF THE CORRECT ANSWER IN THE SPACE AT THE RIGHT.*

1. The one of the following sentences which is LEAST acceptable from the viewpoint of correct usage is: 1.____

    A. The police thought the fugitive to be him.
    B. The criminals set a trap for whoever would fall into it.
    C. It is ten years ago since the fugitive fled from the city.
    D. The lecturer argued that criminals are usually cowards.
    E. The police removed four bucketfuls of earth from the scene of the crime.

2. The one of the following sentences which is LEAST acceptable from the viewpoint of correct usage is: 2.____

    A. The patrolman scrutinized the report with great care.
    B. Approaching the victim of the assault, two bruises were noticed by the patrolman.
    C. As soon as I had broken down the door, I stepped into the room.
    D. I observed the accused loitering near the building, which was closed at the time.
    E. The storekeeper complained that his neighbor was guilty of violating a local ordinance.

3. The one of the following sentences which is LEAST acceptable from the viewpoint of correct usage is: 3.____

    A. I realized immediately that he intended to assault the woman, so I disarmed him.
    B. It was apparent that Mr. Smith's explanation contained many inconsistencies.
    C. Despite the slippery condition of the street, he managed to stop the vehicle before injuring the child.
    D. Not a single one of them wish, despite the damage to property, to make a formal complaint.
    E. The body was found lying on the floor.

4. The one of the following sentences which contains NO error in usage is: 4.____

    A. After the robbers left, the proprietor stood tied in his chair for about two hours before help arrived.
    B. In the cellar I found the watchmans' hat and coat.
    C. The persons living in adjacent apartments stated that they had heard no unusual noises.
    D. Neither a knife or any firearms were found in the room.
    E. Walking down the street, the shouting of the crowd indicated that something was wrong.

5. The one of the following sentences which contains NO error in usage is:

   A. The policeman lay a firm hand on the suspect's shoulder.
   B. It is true that neither strength nor agility are the most important requirement for a good patrolman.
   C. Good citizens constantly strive to do more than merely comply the restraints imposed by society.
   D. No decision was made as to whom the prize should be awarded.
   E. Twenty years is considered a severe sentence for a felony.

6. Which of the following is NOT expressed in standard English usage?

   A. The victim reached a pay-phone booth and manages to call police headquarters.
   B. By the time the call was received, the assailant had left the scene.
   C. The victim has been a respected member of the community for the past eleven years.
   D. Although the lighting was bad and the shadows were deep, the storekeeper caught sight of the attacker.
   E. Additional street lights have since been installed, and the patrols have been strengthened.

7. Which of the following is NOT expressed in standard English usage?

   A. The judge upheld the attorney's right to question the witness about the missing glove.
   B. To be absolutely fair to all parties is the jury's chief responsibility.
   C. Having finished the report, a loud noise in the next room startled the sergeant.
   D. The witness obviously enjoyed having played a part in the proceedings.
   E. The sergeant planned to assign the case to whoever arrived first.

8. In which of the following is a word misused?

   A. As a matter of principle, the captain insisted that the suspect's partner be brought for questioning.
   B. The principle suspect had been detained at the station house for most of the day.
   C. The principal in the crime had no previous criminal record, but his closest associate had been convicted of felonies on two occasions.
   D. The interest payments had been made promptly, but the firm had been drawing upon the principal for these payments.
   E. The accused insisted that his high school principal would furnish him a character reference.

9. Which of the following statements is ambiguous?

   A. Mr. Sullivan explained why Mr. Johnson had been dismissed from his job.
   B. The storekeeper told the patrolman he had made a mistake.
   C. After waiting three hours, the patients in the doctor's office were sent home.
   D. The janitor's duties were to maintain the building in good shape and to answer tenants' complaints.
   E. The speed limit should, in my opinion, be raised to sixty miles an hour on that stretch of road.

10. In which of the following is the punctuation or capitalization faulty? 10._____

   A. The accident occurred at an intersection in the Kew Gardens section of Queens, near the bus stop.
   B. The sedan, not the convertible, was struck in the side.
   C. Before any of the patrolmen had left the police car received an important message from headquarters.
   D. The dog that had been stolen was returned to his master, John Dempsey, who lived in East Village.
   E. The letter had been sent to 12 Hillside Terrace, Rutland, Vermont 05701.

Questions 11-25.

DIRECTIONS: Questions 11 through 25 are to be answered in accordance with correct English usage; that is, standard English rather than nonstandard or substandard. Nonstandard and substandard English includes words or expressions usually classified as slang, dialect, illiterate, etc., which are not generally accepted as correct in current written communication. Standard English also requires clarity, proper punctuation and capitalization and appropriate use of words. Write the letter of the sentence NOT expressed in standard English usage in the space at the right.

11. A. There were three witnesses to the accident. 11._____
    B. At least three witnesses were found to testify for the plaintiff.
    C. Three of the witnesses who took the stand was uncertain about the defendant's competence to drive.
    D. Only three witnesses came forward to testify for the plaintiff.
    E. The three witnesses to the accident were pedestrians.

12. A. The driver had obviously drunk too many martinis before leaving for home. 12._____
    B. The boy who drowned had swum in these same waters many times before.
    C. The petty thief had stolen a bicycle from a private driveway before he was apprehended.
    D. The detectives had brung in the heroin shipment they intercepted.
    E. The passengers had never ridden in a converted bus before.

13. A. Between you and me, the new platoon plan sounds like a good idea. 13._____
    B. Money from an aunt's estate was left to his wife and he.
    C. He and I were assigned to the same patrol for the first time in two months.
    D. Either you or he should check the front door of that store.
    E. The captain himself was not sure of the witness's reliability.

14. A. The alarm had scarcely begun to ring when the explosion occurred. 14._____
    B. Before the firemen arrived on the scene, the second story had been destroyed.
    C. Because of the dense smoke and heat, the firemen could hardly approach the now-blazing structure.
    D. According to the patrolman's report, there wasn't nobody in the store when the explosion occurred.
    E. The sergeant's suggestion was not at all unsound, but no one agreed with him.

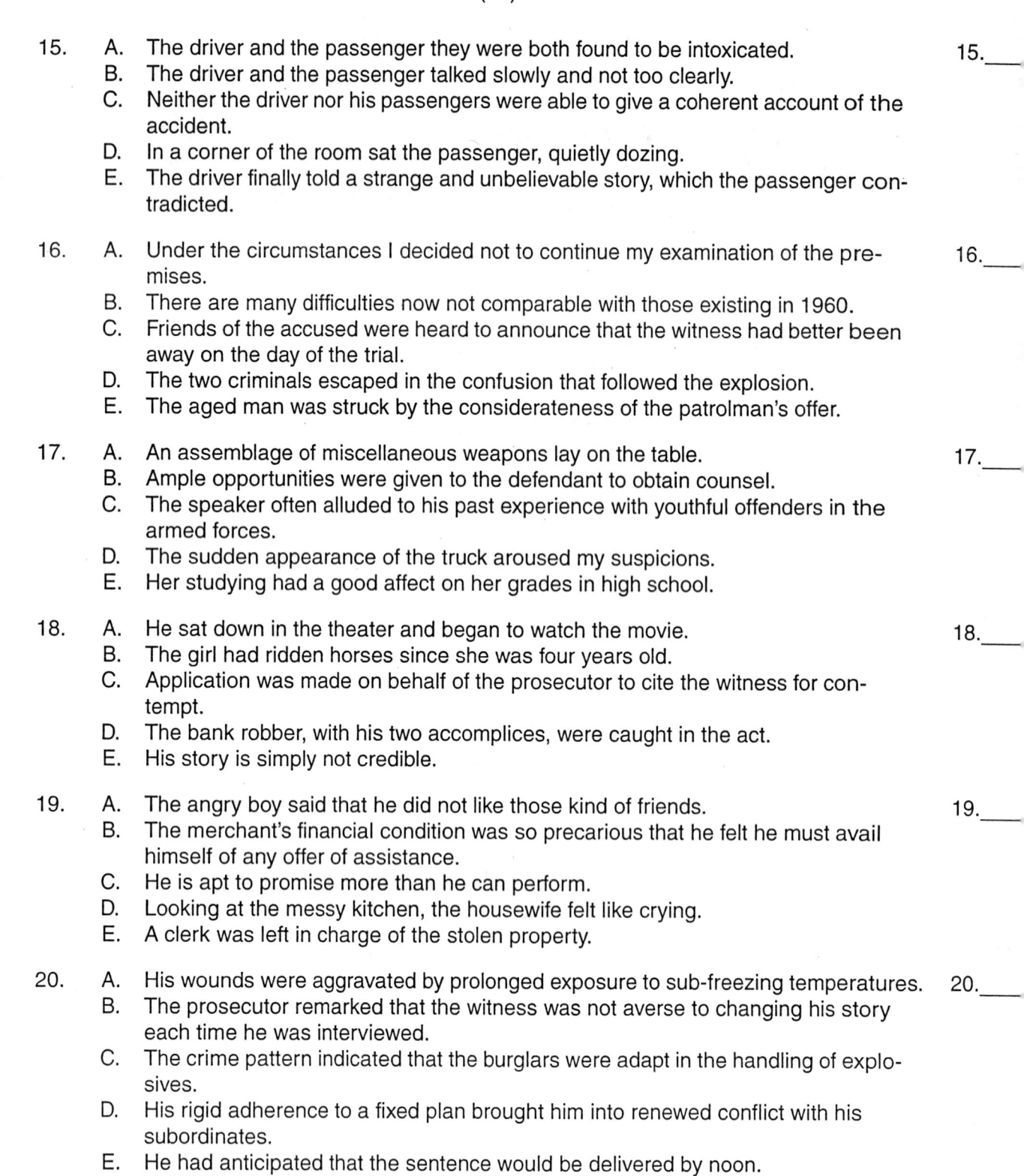

15. A. The driver and the passenger they were both found to be intoxicated.
    B. The driver and the passenger talked slowly and not too clearly.
    C. Neither the driver nor his passengers were able to give a coherent account of the accident.
    D. In a corner of the room sat the passenger, quietly dozing.
    E. The driver finally told a strange and unbelievable story, which the passenger contradicted.

15.___

16. A. Under the circumstances I decided not to continue my examination of the premises.
    B. There are many difficulties now not comparable with those existing in 1960.
    C. Friends of the accused were heard to announce that the witness had better been away on the day of the trial.
    D. The two criminals escaped in the confusion that followed the explosion.
    E. The aged man was struck by the considerateness of the patrolman's offer.

16.___

17. A. An assemblage of miscellaneous weapons lay on the table.
    B. Ample opportunities were given to the defendant to obtain counsel.
    C. The speaker often alluded to his past experience with youthful offenders in the armed forces.
    D. The sudden appearance of the truck aroused my suspicions.
    E. Her studying had a good affect on her grades in high school.

17.___

18. A. He sat down in the theater and began to watch the movie.
    B. The girl had ridden horses since she was four years old.
    C. Application was made on behalf of the prosecutor to cite the witness for contempt.
    D. The bank robber, with his two accomplices, were caught in the act.
    E. His story is simply not credible.

18.___

19. A. The angry boy said that he did not like those kind of friends.
    B. The merchant's financial condition was so precarious that he felt he must avail himself of any offer of assistance.
    C. He is apt to promise more than he can perform.
    D. Looking at the messy kitchen, the housewife felt like crying.
    E. A clerk was left in charge of the stolen property.

19.___

20. A. His wounds were aggravated by prolonged exposure to sub-freezing temperatures.
    B. The prosecutor remarked that the witness was not averse to changing his story each time he was interviewed.
    C. The crime pattern indicated that the burglars were adapt in the handling of explosives.
    D. His rigid adherence to a fixed plan brought him into renewed conflict with his subordinates.
    E. He had anticipated that the sentence would be delivered by noon.

20.___

21. A. The whole arraignment procedure is badly in need of revision. 21.____
     B. After his glasses were broken in the fight, he would of gone to the optometrist if he could.
     C. Neither Tom nor Jack brought his lunch to work.
     D. He stood aside until the quarrel was over.
     E. A statement in the psychiatrist's report disclosed that the probationer vowed to have his revenge.

22. A. His fiery and intemperate speech to the striking employees fatally affected any chance of a future reconciliation. 22.____
     B. The wording of the statute has been variously construed.
     C. The defendant's attorney, speaking in the courtroom, called the official a demagogue who contempuously disregarded the judge's orders.
     D. The baseball game is likely to be the most exciting one this year.
     E. The mother divided the cookies among her two children.

23. A. There was only a bed and a dresser in the dingy room. 23.____
     B. John is one of the few students that have protested the new rule.
     C. It cannot be argued that the child's testimony is negligible; it is, on the contrary, of the greatest importance.
     D. The basic criterion for clearance was so general that officials resolved any doubts in favor of dismissal.
     E. Having just returned from a long vacation, the officer found the city unbearably hot.

24. A. The librarian ought to give more help to small children. 24.____
     B. The small boy was criticized by the teacher because he often wrote careless.
     C. It was generally doubted whether the women would permit the use of her apartment for intelligence operations.
     D. The probationer acts differently every time the officer visits him.
     E. Each of the newly appointed officers has 12 years of service.

25. A. The North is the most industrialized region in the country. 25.____
     B. L. Patrick Gray 3d, the bureau's acting director, stated that, while "rehabilitation is fine" for some convicted criminals, "it is a useless gesture for those who resist every such effort."
     C. Careless driving, faulty mechanism, narrow or badly kept roads all play their part in causing accidents.
     D. The childrens' books were left in the bus.
     E. It was a matter of internal security; consequently, he felt no inclination to rescind his previous order.

KEY (CORRECT ANSWERS)

1.	C	11.	C
2.	B	12.	D
3.	D	13.	B
4.	C	14.	D
5.	E	15.	A
6.	A	16.	C
7.	C	17.	E
8.	B	18.	D
9.	B	19.	A
10.	C	20.	C

21. B
22. E
23. B
24. B
25. D

TEST 2

DIRECTIONS: Each question or incomplete statement is followed by several suggested answers or completions. Select the one that BEST answers the question or completes the statement. *PRINT THE LETTER OF THE CORRECT ANSWER IN THE SPACE AT THE RIGHT.*

Questions 1-6.

DIRECTIONS: Each of Questions 1 through 6 consists of a statement which contains a word (one of those underlined) that is either incorrectly used because it is not in keeping with the meaning the quotation is evidently intended to convey, or is misspelled. There is only one INCORRECT word in each quotation. Of the four underlined words, determine if the first one should be replaced by the word lettered A, the second replaced by the word lettered B, the third replaced by the word lettered C, or the fourth replaced by the word lettered D. *PRINT THE LETTER OF THE REPLACEMENT WORD YOU HAVE SELECTED IN THE SPACE AT THE RIGHT.*

1. Whether one depends on fluorescent or artificial light or both, adequate standards should be maintained by means of systematic tests. 1.____

   A. natural
   B. safeguards
   C. established
   D. routine

2. A policeman has to be prepared to assume his knowledge as a social scientist in the community. 2.____

   A. forced
   B. role
   C. philosopher
   D. street

3. It is practically impossible to indicate whether a sentence is too long simply by measuring its length. 3.____

   A. almost B. tell C. very D. guessing

4. Strong leaders are required to organize a community for delinquency prevention and for dissemination of organized crime and drug addiction. 4.____

   A. tactics B. important C. control D. meetings

5. The demonstrators who were taken to the Criminal Courts building in Manhattan (because it was large enough to accommodate them), contended that the arrests were unwarrented. 5.____

   A. demonstraters
   B. Manhatten
   C. accomodate
   D. unwarranted

6. They were guaranteed a calm atmosphere, free from harrassment, which would be conducive to quiet consideration of the indictments. 6.____

   A. guareenteed
   B. atmospher
   C. harassment
   D. inditements

Questions 7-11.

DIRECTIONS: Each of Questions 7 through 11 consists of a statement containing four words in capital letters. One of these words in capital letters is not in keeping with the meaning which the statement is evidently intended to carry. The four words in capital letters in each statement are reprinted after the statement. Print the capital letter preceding the one of the four words which does MOST to spoil the true meaning of the statement in the space at the right.

7. Retirement and pension systems are essential not only to provide employees with a means of support in the future, but also to prevent longevity and CHARITABLE considerations from UPSETTING the PROMOTIONAL opportunities for RETIRED members of the career service. 7.___

    A. charitable   B. upsetting
    C. promotional   D. retired

8. Within each major DIVISION in a properly set up public or private organization, provision is made so that each NECESSARY activity is CARED for and lines of authority and responsibility are clear-cut and INFINITE. 8.___

    A. division   B. necessary   C. cared   D. infinite

9. In public service, the scale of salaries paid must be INCIDENTAL to the services rendered, with due CONSIDERATION for the attraction of the desired MANPOWER and for the maintenance of a standard of living COMMENSURATE with the work to be performed. 9.___

    A. incidental   B. consideration
    C. manpower   D. commensurate

10. An understanding of the AIMS of an organization by the staff will AID greatly in increasing the DEMAND of the correspondence work of the office, and will to a large extent DETERMINE the nature of the correspondence. 10.___

    A. aims   B. aid   C. demand   D. determine

11. BECAUSE the Civil Service Commission strongly feels that the MERIT system is a key factor in the MAINTENANCE of democratic government, it has adopted as one of its major DEFENSES the progressive democratization of its own procedures in dealing with candidates for positions in the public service. 11.___

    A. Because   B. merit
    C. maintenance   D. defenses

Questions 12-14.

DIRECTIONS: Questions 12 through 14 consist of one sentence each. Each sentence contains an incorrectly used word. First, decide which is the incorrectly used word. Then, from among the options given, decide which word, when substituted for the incorrectly used word, makes the meaning of the sentence clear.

EXAMPLE:
The U.S. national income exhibits a pattern of long term deflection.
A. reflection B. subjection
C. rejoicing D. growth

The word *deflection* in the sentence does not convey the meaning the sentence evidently intended to convey. The word *growth* (Answer D), when substituted for the word *deflection,* makes the meaning of the sentence clear. Accordingly, the answer to the question is D.

12. The study commissioned by the joint committee fell compassionately short of the mark and would have to be redone.

    A. successfully B. insignificantly
    C. experimentally D. woefully

13. He will not idly exploit any violation of the provisions of the order.

    A. tolerate B. refuse C. construe D. guard

14. The defendant refused to be virile and bitterly protested service.

    A. irked B. feasible C. docile D. credible

Questions 15-25.

DIRECTIONS: Questions 15 through 25 consist of short paragraphs. Each paragraph contains one word which is INCORRECTLY used because it is NOT in keeping with the meaning of the paragraph. Find the word in each paragraph which is INCORRECTLY used and then select as the answer the suggested word which should be substituted for the incorrectly used word.

SAMPLE QUESTION:
In determining who is to do the work in your unit, you will have to decide just who does what from day to day. One of your lowest responsibilities is to assign work so that everybody gets a fair share and that everyone can do his part well.
A. new B. old C. important D. performance

EXPLANATION:
The word which is NOT in keeping with the meaning of the paragraph is *lowest*. This is the INCORRECTLY used word. The suggested word *important* would be in keeping with the meaning of the paragraph and should be substituted for *lowest*. Therefore, the CORRECT answer is choice C.

15. If really good practice in the elimination of preventable injuries is to be achieved and held in any establishment, top management must refuse full and definite responsibility and must apply a good share of its attention to the task.

    A. accept B. avoidable C. duties D. problem

16. Recording the human face for identification is by no means the only service performed by the camera in the field of investigation. When the trial of any issue takes place, a word picture is sought to be distorted to the court of incidents, occurrences, or events which are in dispute.

A. appeals B. description
C. portrayed D. deranged

17. In the collection of physical evidence, it cannot be emphasized too strongly that a haphazard systematic search at the scene of the crime is vital. Nothing must be overlooked. Often the only leads in a case will come from the results of this search.

   A. important B. investigation
   C. proof D. thorough

18. If an investigator has reason to suspect that the witness is mentally stable, or a habitual drunkard, he should leave no stone unturned in his investigation to determine if the witness was under the influence of liquor or drugs, or was mentally unbalanced either at the time of the occurrence to which he testified or at the time of the trial.

   A. accused B. clue C. deranged D. question

19. The use of records is a valuable step in crime investigation and is the main reason every department should maintain accurate reports. Crimes are not committed through the use of departmental records alone but from the use of all records, of almost every type, wherever they may be found and whenever they give any incidental information regarding the criminal.

   A. accidental B. necessary
   C. reported D. solved

20. In the years since passage of the Harrison Narcotic Act of 1914, making the possession of opium amphetamines illegal in most circumstances, drug use has become a subject of considerable scientific interest and investigation. There is at present a voluminous literature on drug use of various kinds.

   A. ingestion B. derivatives
   C. addiction D. opiates

21. Of course, the fact that criminal laws are extremely patterned in definition does not mean that the majority of persons who violate them are dealt with as criminals. Quite the contrary, for a great many forbidden acts are voluntarily engaged in within situations of privacy and go unobserved and unreported.

   A. symbolic B. casual
   C. scientific D. broad-gauged

22. The most punitive way to study punishment is to focus attention on the pattern of punitive action: to study how a penalty is applied, to study what is done to or taken from an offender.

   A. characteristic B. degrading
   C. objective D. distinguished

23. The most common forms of punishment in times past have been death, physical torture, mutilation, branding, public humiliation, fines, forfeits of property, banishment, transportation, and imprisonment. Although this list is by no means differentiated, practically every form of punishment has had several variations and applications.

   A. specific B. simple
   C. exhaustive D. characteristic

24. There is another important line of inference between ordinary and professional criminals, and that is the source from which they are recruited. The professional criminal seems to be drawn from legitimate employment and, in many instances, from parallel vocations or pursuits.   24._____

    A. demarcation
    B. justification
    C. superiority
    D. reference

25. He took the position that the success of the program was insidious on getting additional revenue.   25._____

    A. reputed
    B. contingent
    C. failure
    D. indeterminate

KEY (CORRECT ANSWERS)

1.	A	11.	D
2.	B	12.	D
3.	B	13.	A
4.	C	14.	C
5.	D	15.	B
6.	C	16.	A
7.	D	17.	D
8.	D	18.	C
9.	A	19.	D
10.	C	20.	B

21. D
22. C
23. C
24. A
25. B

TEST 3

DIRECTIONS: Each question or incomplete statement is followed by several suggested answers or completions. Select the one that BEST answers the question or completes the statement. *PRINT THE LETTER OF THE CORRECT ANSWER IN THE SPACE AT THE RIGHT.*

Questions 1-5.

DIRECTIONS: Question 1 through 5 are to be answered on the basis of the following:

You are a supervising officer in an investigative unit. Earlier in the day, you directed Detectives Tom Dixon and Sal Mayo to investigate a reported assault and robbery in a liquor store within your area of jurisdiction.

Detective Dixon has submitted to you a preliminary investigative report containing the following information:

- At 1630 hours on 2/20, arrived at Joe's Liquor Store at 350 SW Avenue with Detective Mayo to investigate A & R.
- At store interviewed Rob Ladd, store manager, who stated that he and Joe Brown (store owner) had been stuck up about ten minutes prior to our arrival.
- Ladd described the robbers as male whites in their late teens or early twenties. Further stated that one of the robbers displayed what appeared to be an automatic pistol as he entered the store, and said, *Give us the money or we'll kill you.* Ladd stated that Brown then reached under the counter where he kept a loaded .38 caliber pistol. Several shots followed, and Ladd threw himself to the floor.
- The robbers fled, and Ladd didn't know if any money had been taken.
- At this point, Ladd realized that Brown was unconscious on the floor and bleeding from a head wound.
- Ambulance called by Ladd, and Brown was removed by same to General Hospital.
- Personally interviewed John White, 382 Dartmouth Place, who stated he was inside store at the time of occurrence. White states that he hid behind a wine display upon hearing someone say, *Give us the money.* He then heard shots and saw two young men run from the store to a yellow car parked at the curb. White was unable to further describe auto. States the taller of the two men drove the car away while the other sat on passenger side in front.
- Recovered three spent .38 caliber bullets from premises and delivered them to Crime Lab.
- To General Hospital at 1800 hours but unable to interview Brown, who was under sedation and suffering from shock and a laceration of the head.
- Alarm #12487 transmitted for car and occupants.
- Case Active.

Based solely on the contents of the preliminary investigation submitted by Detective Dixon, select one sentence from the following groups of sentences which is MOST accurate and is grammatically correct.

1. A. Both robbers were armed.
    B. Each of the robbers were described as a male white.
    C. Neither robber was armed.
    D. Mr. Ladd stated that one of the robbers was armed.

2. A. Mr. Brown fired three shots from his revolver.
    B. Mr. Brown was shot in the head by one of the robbers.
    C. Mr. Brown suffered a gunshot wound of the head during the course of the robbery.
    D. Mr. Brown was taken to General Hospital by ambulance.

3. A. Shots were fired after one of the robbers said, *Give us* the money or we'll kill you.
    B. After one of the robbers demanded the money from Mr. Brown, he fired a shot.
    C. The preliminary investigation indicated that although Mr. Brown did not have a license for the gun, he was justified in using deadly physical force.
    D. Mr. Brown was interviewed at General Hospital.

4. A. Each of the witnesses were customers in the store at the time of occurrence.
    B. Neither of the witnesses interviewed was the owner of the liquor store.
    C. Neither of the witnesses interviewed were the owner of the store.
    D. Neither of the witnesses was employed by Mr. Brown.

5. A. Mr. Brown arrived at General Hospital at about 5:00 P.M.
    B. Neither of the robbers was injured during the robbery.
    C. The robbery occurred at 3:30 P.M. on February 10.
    D. One of the witnesses called the ambulance.

Questions 6-10.

DIRECTIONS: Each of Questions 6 through 10 consists of information given in outline form and four sentences labelled A, B, C, and D. For each question, choose the one sentence which CORRECTLY expresses the information given in outline form and which also displays PROPER English usage.

6. Client's Name - Joanna Jones
    Number of Children - 3
    Client's Income - None
    Client's Marital Status - Single

    A. Joanna Jones is an unmarried client with three children who have no income.
    B. Joanna Jones, who is single and has no income, a client she has three children.
    C. Joanna Jones, whose three children are clients, is single and has no income.
    D. Joanna Jones, who has three children, is an unmarried client with no income.

7. Client's Name - Bertha Smith
    Number of Children - 2
    Client's Rent - $105 per month
    Number of Rooms - 4

A. Bertha Smith, a client, pays $105 per month for her four rooms with two children.
B. Client Bertha Smith has two children and pays $105 per month for four rooms.
C. Client Bertha Smith is paying $105 per month for two children with four rooms.
D. For four rooms and two children client Bertha Smith pays $105 per month.

8. Name of Employee - Cynthia Dawes
   Number of Cases Assigned - 9
   Date Cases were Assigned - 12/16
   Number of Assigned Cases Completed - 8

   A. On December 16, employee Cynthia Dawes was assigned nine cases; she has completed eight of these cases.
   B. Cynthia Dawes, employee on December 16, assigned nine cases, completed eight.
   C. Being employed on December 16, Cynthia Dawes completed eight of nine assigned cases.
   D. Employee Cynthia Dawes, she was assigned nine cases and completed eight, on December 16.

8.____

9. Place of Audit - Broadway Center
   Names of Auditors - Paul Cahn, Raymond Perez
   Date of Audit - 11/20
   Number of Cases Audited - 41

   A. On November 20, at the Broadway Center 41 cases was audited by auditors Paul Cahn and Raymond Perez.
   B. Auditors Raymond Perez and Paul Cahn has audited 41 cases at the Broadway Center on November 20.
   C. At the Broadway Center, on November 20, auditors Paul Cahn and Raymond Perez audited 41 cases.
   D. Auditors Paul Cahn and Raymond Perez at the Broadway Center, on November 20, is auditing 41 cases.

9.____

10. Name of Client - Barbra Levine
    Client's Monthly Income - $210
    Client's Monthly Expenses - $452

    A. Barbra Levine is a client, her monthly income is $210 and her monthly expenses is $452.
    B. Barbra Levine's monthly income is $210 and she is a client, with whose monthly expenses are $452.
    C. Barbra Levine is a client whose monthly income is $210 and whose monthly expenses are $452.
    D. Barbra Levine, a client, is with a monthly income which is $210 and monthly expenses which are $452.

10.____

Questions 11-13.

DIRECTIONS: Questions 11 through 13 involve several statements of fact presented in a very simple way. These statements of fact are followed by 4 choices which attempt to incorporate all of the facts into one logical sentence which is properly constructed and grammatically correct.

11.
    I. Mr. Brown was sweeping the sidewalk in front of his house.
    II. He was sweeping it because it was dirty.
    III. He swept the refuse into the street
    IV. Police Officer Green gave him a ticket.
Which one of the following BEST presents the information given above?

    A. Because his sidewalk was dirty, Mr. Brown received a ticket from Officer Green when he swept the refuse into the street.
    B. Police Officer Green gave Mr. Brown a ticket because his sidewalk was dirty and he swept the refuse into the street.
    C. Police Officer Green gave Mr. Brown a ticket for sweeping refuse into the street because his sidewalk was dirty.
    D. Mr. Brown, who was sweeping refuse from his dirty sidewalk into the street, was given a ticket by Police Officer Green.

12.
    I. Sergeant Smith radioed for help.
    II. The sergeant did so because the crowd was getting larger.
    III. It was 10:00 A.M. when he made his call.
    IV. Sergeant Smith was not in uniform at the time of occurrence.
Which one of the following BEST presents the information given above?

    A. Sergeant Smith, although not on duty at the time, radioed for help at 10 o'clock because the crowd was getting uglier.
    B. Although not in uniform, Sergeant Smith called for help at 10:00 A.M. because the crowd was getting uglier.
    C. Sergeant Smith radioed for help at 10:00 A.M. because the crowd was getting larger.
    D. Although he was not in uniform, Sergeant Smith radioed for help at 10:00 A.M. because the crowd was getting larger.

13.
    I. The payroll office is open on Fridays.
    II. Paychecks are distributed from 9:00 A.M. to 12 Noon.
    III. The office is open on Fridays because that's the only day the payroll staff is available.
    IV. It is open for the specified hours in order to permit employees to cash checks at the bank during lunch hour.
The choice below which MOST clearly and accurately presents the above idea is:

    A. Because the payroll office is open on Fridays from 9:00 A.M. to 12 Noon, employees can cash their checks when the payroll staff is available.
    B. Because the payroll staff is only available on Fridays until noon, employees can cash their checks during their lunch hour.
    C. Because the payroll staff is available only on Fridays, the office is open from 9:00 A.M. to 12 Noon to allow employees to cash their checks.
    D. Because of payroll staff availability, the payroll office is open on Fridays. It is open from 9:00 A.M. to 12 Noon so that distributed paychecks can be cashed at the bank while employees are on their lunch hour.

Questions 14-16.

DIRECTIONS: In each of Questions 14 through 16, the four sentences are from a paragraph in a report. They are not in the right order. Which of the following arrangements is the BEST one?

14. I. An executive may answer a letter by writing his reply on the face of the letter itself instead of having a return letter typed.
    II. This procedure is efficient because it saves the executive's time, the typist's time, and saves office file space.
    III. Copying machines are used in small offices as well as large offices to save time and money in making brief replies to business letters.
    IV. A copy is made on a copying machine to go into the company files, while the original is mailed back to the sender.
    The CORRECT answer is:

    A. I, II, IV, III
    B. I, IV, II, III
    C. III, I, IV, II
    D. III, IV, II, I

15. I. Most organizations favor one of the types but always include the others to a lesser degree.
    II. However, we can detect a definite trend toward greater use of symbolic control.
    III. We suggest that our local police agencies are today primarily utilizing material control.
    IV. Control can be classified into three types: physical, material, and symbolic.
    The CORRECT answer is:

    A. IV, II, III, I
    B. II, I, IV, III
    C. III, IV, II, I
    D. IV, I, III, II

16. I. They can and do take advantage of ancient political and geographical boundaries, which often give them sanctuary from effective police activity.
    II. This country is essentially a country of small police forces, each operating independently within the limits of its jurisdiction.
    III. The boundaries that define and limit police operations do not hinder the movement of criminals, of course.
    IV. The machinery of law enforcement in America is fragmented, complicated, and frequently overlapping.
    The CORRECT answer is:

    A. III, I, II, IV
    B. II, IV, I, III
    C. IV, II, III, I
    D. IV, III, II, I

17. Examine the following sentence, and then choose from below the words which should be inserted in the blank spaces to produce the best sentence.
    The unit has exceeded _____ goals and the employees are satisfied with _____ accomplishments.

    A. their, it's
    B. it's, it's
    C. its, there
    D. its, their

18. Examine the following sentence, and then choose from below the words which should be inserted in the blank spaces to produce the best sentence.
Research indicates that employees who _____ no opportunity for close social relationships often find their work unsatisfying, and this _____ of satisfaction often reflects itself in low production.

    A. have, lack
    B. have, excess
    C. has, lack
    D. has, excess

19. Words in a sentence must be arranged properly to make sure that the intended meaning of the sentence is clear. The sentence below that does NOT make sense because a clause has been separated from the word on which its meaning depends is:

    A. To be a good writer, clarity is necessary.
    B. To be a good writer, you must write clearly.
    C. You must write clearly to be a good writer.
    D. Clarity is necessary to good writing.

Questions 20-21.

DIRECTIONS: Each of Questions 20 and 21 consists of a statement which contains a word (one of those underlined) that is either incorrectly used because it is not in keeping with the meaning the quotation is evidently intended to convey, or is misspelled. There is only one INCORRECT word in each quotation. Of the four underlined words, determine if the first one should be replaced by the word lettered A, the second one replaced by the word lettered B, the third one replaced by the word lettered C, or the fourth one replaced by the word lettered D. *PRINT THE LETTER OF THE REPLACEMENT WORD YOU HAVE SELECTED IN THE SPACE AT THE RIGHT.*

20. The alleged killer was occasionally permitted to excercise in the corridor.

    A. alledged
    B. ocasionally
    C. permited
    D. exercise

21. Defense counsel stated, in affect, that their conduct was permissible under the First Amendment.

    A. council
    B. effect
    C. there
    D. permissable

Question 22.

DIRECTIONS: Question 22 consists of one sentence. This sentence contains an incorrectly used word. First, decide which is the incorrectly used word. Then, from among the options given, decide which word, when substituted for the incorrectly used word, makes the meaning of the sentence clear.

22. As today's violence has no single cause, so its causes have no single scheme.

    A. deference   B. cure   C. flaw   D. relevance

23. In the sentence, *A man in a light-grey suit waited thirty-five minutes in the ante-room for the all-important document,* the word IMPROPERLY hyphenated is

    A. light-grey
    B. thirty-five
    C. ante-room
    D. all-important

24. In the sentence, *The candidate wants to file his application for preference before it is too late,* the word *before* is used as a(n)

    A. preposition
    B. subordinating conjunction
    C. pronoun
    D. adverb

25. In the sentence, *The perpetrators ran from the scene,* the word *from* is a

    A. preposition
    B. pronoun
    C. verb
    D. conjunction

KEY (CORRECT ANSWERS)

1.	D	11.	D
2.	D	12.	D
3.	A	13.	D
4.	B	14.	C
5.	D	15.	D
6.	D	16.	C
7.	B	17.	D
8.	A	18.	A
9.	C	19.	A
10.	C	20.	D

21. B
22. B
23. C
24. B
25. A

PREPARING WRITTEN MATERIAL

EXAMINATION SECTION
TEST 1

Questions 1-15.

DIRECTIONS: For each of Questions 1 through 15, select from the options given below the MOST applicable choice, and mark your answer accordingly.

    A. The sentence is correct.
    B. The sentence contains a spelling error *only*.
    C. The sentence contains an English grammar error *only*.
    D. The sentence contains both a spelling error and an English grammar error.

1. He is a very dependible person whom we expect will be an asset to this division.   1.____
2. An investigator often finds it necessary to be very diplomatic when conducting an interview.   2.____
3. Accurate detail is especially important if court action results from an investigation.   3.____
4. The report was signed by him and I since we conducted the investigation jointly.   4.____
5. Upon receipt of the complaint, an inquiry was begun.   5.____
6. An employee has to organize his time so that he can handle his workload efficiantly.   6.____
7. It was not apparant that anyone was living at the address given by the client.   7.____
8. According to regulations, there is to be at least three attempts made to locate the client.   8.____
9. Neither the inmate nor the correction officer was willing to sign a formal statement.   9.____
10. It is our opinion that one of the persons interviewed were lying.   10.____
11. We interviewed both clients and departmental personel in the course of this investigation.   11.____
12. It is concievable that further research might produce additional evidence.   12.____
13. There are too many occurences of this nature to ignore.   13.____
14. We cannot accede to the candidate's request.   14.____
15. The submission of overdue reports is the reason that there was a delay in completion of this investigation.   15.____

Questions 16-25.

DIRECTIONS: Each of Questions 16 through 25 may be classified under one of the following four categories:

    A. Faulty because of incorrect grammar or sentence structure
    B. Faulty because of incorrect punctuation
    C. Faulty because of incorrect spelling
    D. Correct

Examine each sentence carefully to determine under which of the above four options it is best classified. Then, in the space at the right, write the letter preceding the option which is the BEST of the four suggested above. Each incorrect sentence contains but one type of error. Consider a sentence to be correct if it contains none of the types of errors mentioned, even though there may be other correct ways of expressing the same thought.

16. Although the department's supply of scratch pads and stationary have diminished considerably, the allotment for our division has not been reduced.   16.___

17. You have not told us whom you wish to designate as your secretary.   17.___

18. Upon reading the minutes of the last meeting, the new proposal was taken up for consideration.   18.___

19. Before beginning the discussion, we locked the door as a precautionery measure.   19.___

20. The supervisor remarked, "Only those clerks, who perform routine work, are permitted to take a rest period."   20.___

21. Not only will this duplicating machine make accurate copies, but it will also produce a quantity of work equal to fifteen transcribing typists.   21.___

22. "Mr. Jones," said the supervisor, "we regret our inability to grant you an extention of your leave of absence."   22.___

23. Although the employees find the work monotonous and fatigueing, they rarely complain.   23.___

24. We completed the tabulation of the receipts on time despite the fact that Miss Smith our fastest operator was absent for over a week.   24.___

25. The reaction of the employees who attended the meeting, as well as the reaction of those who did not attend, indicates clearly that the schedule is satisfactory to everyone concerned.   25.___

KEY (CORRECT ANSWERS)

1.	D	11.	B
2.	A	12.	B
3.	A	13.	B
4.	C	14.	A
5.	A	15.	C
6.	B	16.	A
7.	B	17.	D
8.	C	18.	A
9.	A	19.	C
10.	C	20.	B

21. A
22. C
23. C
24. B
25. D

TEST 2

Questions 1-15.

DIRECTIONS: Questions 1 through 15 consist of two sentences. Some are correct according to ordinary formal English usage. Others are incorrect because they contain errors in English usage, spelling, or punctuation. Consider a sentence correct if it contains no errors in English usage, spelling, or punctuation, even if there may be other ways of writing the sentence correctly. Mark your answer:

A. If only sentence I is correct
B. If only sentence II is correct
C. If sentences I and II are correct
D. If neither sentence I nor II is correct

1. I. The influence of recruitment efficiency upon administrative standards is readily apparant.
   II. Rapid and accurate thinking are an essential quality of the police officer.

2. I. The administrator of a police department is constantly confronted by the demands of subordinates for increased personnel in their respective units.
   II. Since a chief executive must work within well-defined fiscal limits, he must weigh the relative importance of various requests.

3. I. The two men whom the police arrested for a parking violation were wanted for robbery in three states.
   II. Strong executive control from the top to the bottom of the enterprise is one of the basic principals of police administration.

4. I. When he gave testimony unfavorable to the defendant loyalty seemed to mean very little.
   II. Having run off the road while passing a car, the patrolman gave the driver a traffic ticket.

5. I. The judge ruled that the defendant's conversation with his doctor was a priviliged communication.
   II. The importance of our training program is widely recognized; however, fiscal difficulties limit the program's effectiveness.

6. I. Despite an increase in patrol coverage, there were less arrests for crimes against property this year.
   II. The investigators could hardly have expected greater cooperation from the public.

7. I. Neither the patrolman nor the witness could identify the defendant as the driver of the car.
   II. Each of the officers in the class received their certificates at the completion of the course.

8. I. The new commander made it clear that those kind of procedures would no longer be permitted.   8._____
    II. Giving some weight to performance records is more advisable then making promotions solely on the basis of test scores.

9. I. A deputy sheriff must ascertain whether the debtor, has any property.   9._____
    II. A good deputy sheriff does not cause histerical excitement when he executes a process.

10. I. Having learned that he has been assigned a judgment debtor, the deputy sheriff should call upon him.   10._____
    II. The deputy sheriff may seize and remove property without requiring a bond.

11. I. If legal procedures are not observed, the resulting contract is not enforseable.   11._____
    II. If the directions from the creditor's attorney are not in writing, the deputy sheriff should request a letter of instructions from the attorney.

12. I. The deputy sheriff may confer with the defendant and may enter this defendants' place of business.   12._____
    II. A deputy sheriff must ascertain from the creditor's attorney whether the debtor has any property against which he may proceede.

13. I. The sheriff has a right to do whatever is reasonably necessary for the purpose of executing the order of the court.   13._____
    II. The written order of the court gives the sheriff general authority and he is governed in his acts by a very simple principal.

14. I. Either the patrolman or his sergeant are always ready to help the public.   14._____
    II. The sergeant asked the patrolman when he would finish the report.

15. I. The injured man could not hardly talk.   15._____
    II. Every officer had ought to hand in their reports on time.

Questions 16-25.

DIRECTIONS: For each of the sentences given below, numbered 16 through 25, select from the following choices the MOST correct choice and print your choice in the space at the right. Select as your answer:

  A. If the statement contains an unnecessary word or expression
  B. If the statement contains a slang term or expression ordinarily not acceptable in government report writing
  C. If the statement contains an old-fashioned word or expression, where a concrete, plain term would be more useful
  D. If the statement contains no major faults

16. Every one of us should try harder   16._____

17. Yours of the first instant has been received.   17._____

18. We will have to do a real snow job on him.   18._____

19. I shall contact him next Thursday.   19._____

20. None of us were invited to the meeting with the community. 20.____
21. We got this here job to do. 21.____
22. She could not help but see the mistake in the checkbook. 22.____
23. Don't bug the Director about the report. 23.____
24. I beg to inform you that your letter has been received. 24.____
25. This project is all screwed up. 25.____

KEY (CORRECT ANSWERS)

1.	D	11.	B
2.	C	12.	D
3.	A	13.	A
4.	D	14.	D
5.	B	15.	D
6.	B	16.	D
7.	A	17.	C
8.	D	18.	B
9.	D	19.	D
10.	C	20.	D

21. B
22. D
23. B
24. C
25. B

TEST 3

DIRECTIONS: Questions 1 through 25 are sentences taken from reports. Some are correct according to ordinary formal English usage. Others are incorrect because they contain errors in English usage, spelling, or punctuation. Consider a sentence correct if it contains no errors in English usage, spelling, or punctuation, even if there may be other ways of writing the sentence correctly. Mark your answer:

    A. If only sentence I is correct
    B. If only sentence II is correct
    C. If sentences I and II are correct
    D. If neither sentence I nor II is correct.

1.
   I. The Neighborhood Police Team Commander and Team Patrol- men are encouraged to give to the public the widest possible verbal and written disemination of information regarding the existence and purposes of the program.
   II. The police must be vitally interelated with every segment of the public they serve.

2.
   I. If social gambling, prostitution, and other vices are to be prohibited, the law makers should provide the manpower and method for enforcement.
   II. In addition to checking on possible crime locations such as hallways, roofs yards and other similar locations, Team Patrolmen are encouraged to make known their presence to members of the community.

3.
   I. The Neighborhood Police Team Commander is authorized to secure, the cooperation of local publications, as well as public and private agencies, to further the goals of the program.
   II. Recruitment from social minorities is essential to effective police work among minorities and meaningful relations with them.

4.
   I. The Neighborhood Police Team Commander and his men have the responsibility for providing patrol service within the sector territory on a twenty-four hour basis.
   II. While the patrolman was walking his beat at midnight he noticed that the clothing stores' door was partly open.

5.
   I. Authority is granted to the Neighborhood Police Team to device tactics for coping with the crime in the sector.
   II. Before leaving the scene of the accident, the patrolman drew a map showing the positions of the automobiles and indicated the time of the accident as 10 M. in the morning.

6.
   I. The Neighborhood Police Team Commander and his men must be kept apprised of conditions effecting their sector.
   II. Clear, continuous communication with every segment of the public served based on the realization of mutual need and founded on trust and confidence is the basis for effective law enforcement.

7.
  I. The irony is that the police are blamed for the laws they enforce when they are doing their duty.
  II. The Neighborhood Police Team Commander is authorized to prepare and distribute literature with pertinent information telling the public whom to contact for assistance.

8.
  I. The day is not far distant when major parts of the entire police compliment will need extensive college training or degrees.
  II. Although driving under the influence of alcohol is a specific charge in making arrests, drunkeness is basically a health and social problem.

9.
  I. If a deputy sheriff finds that property he has to attach is located on a ship, he should notify his supervisor.
  II. Any contract that tends to interfere with the administration of justice is illegal.

10.
  I. A mandate or official order of the court to the sheriff or other officer directs it to take into possession property of the judgment debtor.
  II. Tenancies from month-to-month, week-to-week, and sometimes year-to-year are termenable.

11.
  I. A civil arrest is an arrest pursuant to an order issued by a court in civil litigation.
  II. In a criminal arrest, a defendant is arrested for a crime he is alleged to have committed.

12.
  I. Having taken a defendant into custody, there is a complete restraint of personal liberty.
  II. Actual force is unnecessary when a deputy sheriff makes an arrest.

13.
  I. When a husband breaches a separation agreement by failing to supply to the wife the amount of money to be paid to her periodically under the agreement, the same legal steps may be taken to enforce his compliance as in any other breach of contract.
  II. Having obtained the writ of attachment, the plaintiff is then in the advantageous position of selling the very property that has been held for him by the sheriff while he was obtaining a judgment.

14.
  I. Being locked in his desk, the investigator felt sure that the records would be safe.
  II. The reason why the witness changed his statement was because he had been threatened.

15.
  I. The investigation had just began then an important witness disappeared.
  II. The check that had been missing was located and returned to its owner, Harry Morgan, a resident of Suffolk County, New York.

16.
  I. A supervisor will find that the establishment of standard procedures enables his staff to work more efficiently.
  II. An investigator hadn't ought to give any recommendations in his report if he is in doubt.

17.
  I. Neither the investigator nor his supervisor is ready to interview the witnesses.
  II. Interviewing has been and always will be an important asset in investigation.

18. I. One of the investigator's reports has been forwarded to the wrong person.
    II. The investigator stated that he was not familiar with those kind of cases.

19. I. Approaching the victim of the assault, two large bruises were noticed by me.
    II. The prisoner was arrested for assault, resisting arrest, and use of a deadly weapon.

20. I. A copy of the orders, which had been prepared by the captain, was given to each patrolman.
    II. It's always necessary to inform an arrested person of his constitutional rights before asking him any questions.

21. I. To prevent further bleeding, I applied a tourniquet to the wound.
    II. John Rano a senior officer was on duty at the time of the accident.

22. I. Limiting the term "property" to tangible property, in the criminal mischief setting, accords with prior case law holding that only tangible property came within the purview of the offense of malicious mischief.
    II. Thus, a person who intentionally destroys the property of another, but under an honest belief that he has title to such property, cannot be convicted of criminal mischief under the Revised Penal Law.

23. I. Very early in it's history, New York enacted statutes from time to time punishing, either as a felony or as a misdemeanor, malicious injuries to various kinds of property: piers, booms, dams, bridges, etc.
    II. The application of the statute is necessarily restricted to trespassory takings with larcenous intent: namely with intent permanently or virtually permanently to "appropriate" property or "deprive" the owner of its use.

24. I. Since the former Penal Law did not define the instruments of forgery in a general fashion, its crime of forgery was held to be narrower than the common law offense in this respect and to embrace only those instruments explicitly specified in the substantive provisions.
    II. After entering the barn through an open door for the purpose of stealing, it was closed by the defendants.

25. I. The use of fire or explosives to destroy tangible property is proscribed by the criminal mischief provisions of the Revised Penal Law.
    II. The defendant's taking of a taxicab for the immediate purpose of affecting his escape did not constitute grand larceny.

KEY (CORRECT ANSWERS)

1. D
2. D
3. B
4. A
5. D

6. D
7. C
8. D
9. C
10. D

11. C
12. B
13. C
14. D
15. B

16. A
17. C
18. A
19. B
20. C

21. A
22. C
23. B
24. A
25. A

TEST 4

Questions 1-4.

DIRECTIONS: Each of the two sentences in Questions 1 through 4 may be correct or may contain errors in punctuation, capitalization, or grammar. Mark your answer:

    A. If there is an error only in sentence I
    B. If there is an error only in sentence II
    C. If there is an error in both sentences I and II
    D. If both sentences are correct.

1.   I. It is very annoying to have a pencil sharpener, which is not in working order.
    II. Patrolman Blake checked the door of Joe's Restaurant and found that the lock has been jammed.

2.   I. When you are studying a good textbook is important.
    II. He said he would divide the money equally between you and me.

3.   I. Since he went on the city council a year ago, one of his primary concerns has been safety in the streets.
    II. After waiting in the doorway for about 15 minutes, a black sedan appeared.

Questions 5-9.

DIRECTIONS: Each of the sentences in Questions 5 through 9 may be classified under one of the following four categories:
    A. Faulty because of incorrect grammar
    B. Faulty because of incorrect punctuation
    C. Faulty because of incorrect capitalization or incorrect spelling
    D. Correct

Examine each sentence carefully to determine under which of the above four options it is BEST classified. Then, in the space at the right, print the capitalized letter preceding the option which is the BEST of the four suggested above. Each faulty sentence contains but one type of error. Consider a sentence to be correct if it contains none of the types of errors mentioned, even though there may be other correct ways of expressing the same thought.

5. They told both he and I that the prisoner had escaped.

6. Any superior officer, who, disregards the just complaints of his subordinates, is remiss in the performance of his duty.

7. Only those members of the national organization who resided in the Middle west attended the conference in Chicago.

8. We told him to give the investigation assignment to whoever was available.

9. Please do not disappoint and embarass us by not appearing in court.

Questions 10-14.

DIRECTIONS: Each of Questions 10 through 14 consists of three sentences lettered A, B, and C. In each of these questions, one of the sentences may contain an error in grammar, sentence structure, or punctuation, or all three sentences may be correct. If one of the sentences in a question contains an error in grammar, sentence structure, or punctuation, print in the space at the right the capital letter preceding the sentence which contains the error. If all three sentences are correct, print the letter D.

10. A. Mr. Smith appears to be less competent than I in performing these duties. 10.___
    B. The supervisor spoke to the employee, who had made the error, but did not reprimand him.
    C. When he found the book lying on the table, he immediately notified the owner.

11. A. Being locked in the desk, we were certain that the papers would not be taken. 11.___
    B. It wasn't I who dictated the telegram; I believe it was Eleanor.
    C. You should interview whoever comes to the office today.

12. A. The clerk was instructed to set the machine on the table before summoning the manager. 12.___
    B. He said that he was not familiar with those kind of activities.
    C. A box of pencils, in addition to erasers and blotters, was included in the shipment of supplies.

13. A. The supervisor remarked, "Assigning an employee to the proper type of work is not always easy." 13.___
    B. The employer found that each of the applicants were qualified to perform the duties of the position.
    C. Any competent student is permitted to take this course if he obtains the consent of the instructor.

14. A. The prize was awarded to the employee whom the judges believed to be most deserving. 14.___
    B. Since the instructor believes this book is the better of the two, he is recommending it for use in the school.
    C. It was obvious to the employees that the completion of the task by the scheduled date would require their working overtime.

Questions 15-21.

DIRECTIONS: In answering Questions 15 through 21, choose the sentence which is BEST from the point of view of English usage suitable for a business report.

15. A. The client's receiving of public assistance checks at two different addresses were disclosed by the investigation.
     B. The investigation disclosed that the client was receiving public assistance checks at two different addresses.
     C. The client was found out by the investigation to be receiving public assistance checks at two different addresses.
     D. The client has been receiving public assistance checks at two different addresses, disclosed the investigation.

15.____

16. A. The investigation of complaints are usually handled by this unit, which deals with internal security problems in the department.
     B. This unit deals with internal security problems in the department usually investigating complaints.
     C. Investigating complaints is this unit's job, being that it handles internal security problems in the department.
     D. This unit deals with internal security problems in the department and usually investigates complaints.

16.____

17. A. The delay in completing this investigation was caused by difficulty in obtaining the required documents from the candidate.
     B. Because of difficulty in obtaining the required documents from the candidate is the reason that there was a delay in completing this investigation.
     C. Having had difficulty in obtaining the required documents from the candidate, there was a delay in completing this investigation.
     D. Difficulty in obtaining the required documents from the candidate had the affect of delaying the completion of this investigation.

17.____

18. A. This report, together with documents supporting our recommendation, are being submitted for your approval.
     B. Documents supporting our recommendation is being submitted with the report for your approval.
     C. This report, together with documents supporting our recommendation, is being submitted for your approval.
     D. The report and documents supporting our recommendation is being submitted for your approval.

18.____

19. A. The chairman himself, rather than his aides, has reviewed the report.
     B. The chairman himself, rather than his aides, have reviewed the report.
     C. The chairmen, not the aide, has reviewed the report.
     D. The aide, not the chairmen, have reviewed the report.

19.____

20. A. Various proposals were submitted but the decision is not been made.
     B. Various proposals has been submitted but the decision has not been made.
     C. Various proposals were submitted but the decision is not been made.
     D. Various proposals have been submitted but the decision has not been made.

20.____

21. A. Everyone were rewarded for his successful attempt.
     B. They were successful in their attempts and each of them was rewarded.
     C. Each of them are rewarded for their successful attempts.
     D. The reward for their successful attempts were made to each of them.

21.____

22. The following is a paragraph from a request for departmental recognition consisting of five numbered sentences submitted to a Captain for review. These sentences may or may not have errors in spelling, grammar, and punctuation:

    1. The officers observed the subject Mills surreptitiously remove a wallet from the woman's handbag and entered his automobile. 2. As they approached Mills, he looked in their direction and drove away. 3. The officers pursued in their car. 4. Mills executed a series of complicated manuvers to evade the pursuing officers. 5. At the corner of Broome and Elizabeth Streets, Mills stopped the car, got out, raised his hands and surrendered to the officers.

    Which one of the following BEST classifies the above with regard to spelling, grammar and punctuation?

    A. 1, 2, and 3 are correct, but 4 and 5 have errors.
    B. 2, 3, and 5 are correct, but 1 and 4 have errors.
    C. 3, 4, and 5 are correct, but 1 and 2 have errors.
    D. 1, 2, 3, and 5 are correct, but 4 has errors.

23. The one of the following sentences which is grammatically PREFERABLE to the others is:

    A. Our engineers will go over your blueprints so that you may have no problems in construction.
    B. For a long time he had been arguing that we, not he, are to blame for the confusion.
    C. I worked on this automobile for two hours and still cannot find out what is wrong with it.
    D. Accustomed to all kinds of hardships, fatigue seldom bothers veteran policemen.

24. The MOST accurate of the following sentences is:

    A. The commissioner, as well as his deputy and various bureau heads, were present.
    B. A new organization of employers and employees have been formed.
    C. One or the other of these men have been selected.
    D. The number of pages in the book is enough to discourage a reader.

25. The MOST accurate of the following sentences is:

    A. Between you and me, I think he is the better man.
    B. He was believed to be me.
    C. Is it us that you wish to see?
    D. The winners are him and her.

KEY (CORRECT ANSWERS)

1. C
2. A
3. C
4. B
5. A

6. B
7. C
8. D
9. C
10. B

11. A
12. B
13. B
14. D
15. B

16. D
17. A
18. C
19. A
20. D

21. B
22. B
23. A
24. D
25. A

PREPARING WRITTEN MATERIAL

PARAGRAPH REARRANGEMENT
COMMENTARY

The sentences which follow are in scrambled order. You are to rearrange them in proper order and indicate the letter choice containing the correct answer at the space at the right.

Each group of sentences in this section is actually a paragraph presented in scrambled order. Each sentence in the group has a place in that paragraph; no sentence is to be left out. You are to read each group of sentences and decide upon the best order in which to put the sentences so as to form as well-organized paragraph.

The questions in this section measure the ability to solve a problem when all the facts relevant to its solution are not given.

More specifically, certain positions of responsibility and authority require the employee to discover connections between events sometimes, apparently, unrelated. In order to do this, the employee will find it necessary to correctly infer that unspecified events have probably occurred or are likely to occur. This ability becomes especially important when action must be taken on incomplete information.

Accordingly, these questions require competitors to choose among several suggested alternatives, each of which presents a different sequential arrangement of the events. Competitors must choose the MOST logical of the suggested sequences.

In order to do so, they may be required to draw on general knowledge to infer missing concepts or events that are essential to sequencing the given events. Competitors should be careful to infer only what is essential to the sequence. The plausibility of the wrong alternatives will always require the inclusion of unlikely events or of additional chains of events which are NOT essential to sequencing the given events.

It's very important to remember that you are looking for the best of the four possible choices, and that the best choice of all may not even be one of the answers you're given to choose from.

There is no one right way to these problems. Many people have found it helpful to first write out the order of the sentences, as they would have arranged them, on their scrap paper before looking at the possible answers. If their optimum answer is there, this can save them some time. If it isn't, this method can still give insight into solving the problem. Others find it most helpful to just go through each of the possible choices, contrasting each as they go along. You should use whatever method feels comfortable, and works, for you.

While most of these types of questions are not that difficult, we've added a higher percentage of the difficult type, just to give you more practice. Usually there are only one or two questions on this section that contain such subtle distinctions that you're unable to answer confidently, and you then may find yourself stuck deciding between two possible choices, neither of which you're sure about.

EXAMINATION SECTION
TEST 1

DIRECTIONS: Each question consists of several sentences which can be arranged in a logical sequence. For each question, select the choice which places the numbered sentences in the MOST logical sequence. *PRINT THE LETTER OF THE CORRECT ANSWER IN THE SPACE AT THE RIGHT.*

1. I. A body was found in the woods.
    II. A man proclaimed innocence.
    III. The owner of a gun was located.
    IV. A gun was traced.
    V. The owner of a gun was questioned.
    The CORRECT answer is:

    A. IV, III, V, II, I B. II, I, IV, III, V
    C. I, IV, III, V, II D. I, III, V, II, IV
    E. I, II, IV, III, V

    1.____

2. I. A man was in a hunting accident.
    II. A man fell down a flight of steps.
    III. A man lost his vision in one eye.
    IV. A man broke his leg.
    V. A man had to walk with a cane.
    The CORRECT answer is:

    A. II, IV, V, I, III B. IV, V, I, III, II
    C. III, I, IV, V, II D. I, III, V, II, IV
    E. I, III, II, IV, V

    2.____

3. I. A man is offered a new job.
    II. A woman is offered a new job.
    III. A man works as a waiter.
    IV. A woman works as a waitress.
    V. A woman gives notice.
    The CORRECT answer is:

    A. IV, II, V, III, I B. IV, II, V, I, III
    C. II, IV, V, III, I D. III, I, IV, II, V
    E. IV, III, II, V, I

    3.____

4. I. A train left the station late.
    II. A man was late for work.
    III. A man lost his job.
    IV. Many people complained because the train was late.
    V. There was a traffic jam.
    The CORRECT answer is:

    A. V, II, I, IV, III B. V, I, IV, II, III
    C. V, I, II, IV, III D. I, V, IV, II, III
    E. II, I, IV, V, III

    4.____

2 (#1)

5.
   I. The burden of proof as to each issue is determined before trial and remains upon the same party throughout the trial.
   II. The jury is at liberty to believe one witness' testimony as against a number of contradictory witnesses.
   III. In a civil case, the party bearing the burden of proof is required to prove his contention by a fair preponderance of the evidence.
   IV. However, it must be noted that a fair preponderance of evidence does not necessarily mean a greater number of witnesses.
   V. The burden of proof is the burden which rests upon one of the parties to an action to persuade the trier of the facts, generally the jury, that a proposition he asserts is true.
   VI. If the evidence is equally balanced, or if it leaves the jury in such doubt as to be unable to decide the controversy either way, judgment must be given against the party upon whom the burden of proof rests.

   The CORRECT answer is:

   A. III, II, V, IV, I, VI
   B. I, II, VI, V, III, IV
   C. III, IV, V, I, II, VI
   D. V, I, III, VI, IV, II
   E. I, V, III, VI, IV, II

6.
   I. If a parent is without assets and is unemployed, he cannot be convicted of the crime of non-support of a child.
   II. The term *sufficient ability* has been held to mean sufficient financial ability.
   III. It does not matter if his unemployment is by choice or unavoidable circumstances.
   IV. If he fails to take any steps at all, he may be liable to prosecution for endangering the welfare of a child.
   V. Under the penal law, a parent is responsible for the support of his minor child only if the parent is *of* sufficient ability.
   VI. An indigent parent may meet his obligation by borrowing money or by seeking aid under the provisions of the Social Welfare Law.

   The CORRECT answer is:

   A. VI, I, V, III, II, IV
   B. I, III, V, II, IV, VI
   C. V, II, I, III, VI, IV
   D. I, VI, IV, V, II, III
   E. II, V, I, III, VI, IV

7.
   I. Consider, for example, the case of a rabble rouser who urges a group of twenty people to go out and break the windows of a nearby factory.
   II. Therefore, the law fills the indicated gap with the crime of *inciting to riot*.
   III. A person is considered guilty of inciting to riot when he urges ten or more persons to engage in tumultuous and violent conduct of a kind likely to create public alarm.
   IV. However, if he has not obtained the cooperation of at least four people, he cannot be charged with unlawful assembly.
   V. The charge of inciting to riot was added to the law to cover types of conduct which cannot be classified as either the crime of *riot* or the crime of *unlawful assembly*.
   VI. If he acquires the acquiescence of at least four of them, he is guilty of unlawful assembly even if the project does not materialize.

   The CORRECT answer is:

A. III, V, I, VI, IV, II		B. V, I, IV, VI, II, III	
C. III, IV, I, V, II, VI		D. V, I, IV, VI, III, II	
E. V, III, I, VI, IV, II			

8. I. If, however, the rebuttal evidence presents an issue of credibility, it is for the jury to determine whether the presumption has, in fact, been destroyed.
    II. Once sufficient evidence to the contrary is introduced, the presumption disappears from the trial.
    III. The effect of a presumption is to place the burden upon the adversary to come forward with evidence to rebut the presumption.
    IV. When a presumption is overcome and ceases to exist in the case, the fact or facts which gave rise to the presumption still remain.
    V. Whether a presumption has been overcome is ordinarily a question for the court.
    VI. Such information may furnish a basis for a logical inference.
    The CORRECT answer is:

    A. IV, VI, II, V, I, III   B. III, II, V, I, IV, VI
    C. V, III, VI, IV, II, I   D. V, IV, I, II, VI, III
    E. II, III, V, I, IV, VI

9. I. An executive may answer a letter by writing his reply on the face of the letter itself instead of having a return letter typed.
    II. This procedure is efficient because it saves the executive's time, the typist's time, and saves office file space.
    III. Copying machines are used in small offices as well as large offices to save time and money in making brief replies to business letters.
    IV. A copy is made on a copying machine to go into the company files, while the original is mailed back to the sender.
    The CORRECT answer is:

    A. I, II, IV, III   B. I, IV, II, III
    C. III, I, IV, II   D. III, IV, II, I

10. I. Most organizations favor one of the types but always include the others to a lesser degree.
    II. However, we can detect a definite trend toward greater use of symbolic control.
    III. We suggest that our local police agencies are today primarily utilizing material control.
    IV. Control can be classified into three types: physical, material, and symbolic.
    The CORRECT answer is:

    A. IV, II, III, I   B. II, I, IV, III
    C. III, IV, II, I   D. IV, I, III, II

11. I. Project residents had first claim to this use, followed by surrounding neighborhood children.
    II. By contrast, recreation space within the project's interior was found to be used more often by both groups.
    III. Studies of the use of project grounds in many cities showed grounds left open for public use were neglected and unused, both by residents and by members of the surrounding community.

IV. Project residents had clearly laid claim to the play spaces, setting up and enforcing unwritten rules for use.
V. Each group, by experience, found their activities easily disrupted by other groups, and their claim to the use of space for recreation difficult to enforce.

The CORRECT answer is:

A. IV, V, I, II, III
B. V, II, IV, III, I
C. I, IV, III, II, V
D. III, V, II, IV, I

12.
I. They do not consider the problems correctable within the existing subsidy formula and social policy of accepting all eligible applicants regardless of social behavior and lifestyle.
II. A recent survey, however, indicated that tenants believe these problems correctable by local housing authorities and management within the existing financial formula.
III. Many of the problems and complaints concerning public housing management and design have created resentment between the tenant and the landlord.
IV. This same survey indicated that administrators and managers do not agree with the tenants.

The CORRECT answer is:

A. II, I, III, IV
B. I, III, IV, II
C. III, II, IV, I
D. IV, II, I, III

13.
I. In single-family residences, there is usually enough distance between tenants to prevent occupants from annoying one another.
II. For example, a certain small percentage of tenant families has one or more members addicted to alcohol.
III. While managers believe in the right of individuals to live as they choose, the manager becomes concerned when the pattern of living jeopardizes others' rights.
IV. Still others turn night into day, staging lusty entertainments which carry on into the hours when most tenants are trying to sleep.
V. In apartment buildings, however, tenants live so closely together that any misbehavior can result in unpleasant living conditions.
VI. Other families engage in violent argument.

The CORRECT answer is:

A. III, II, V, IV, VI, I
B. I, V, II, VI, IV, III
C. II, V, IV, I, III, VI
D. IV, II, V, VI, III, I

14.
I. Congress made the commitment explicit in the Housing Act of 1949, establishing as a national goal the realization of *a decent home and suitable environment for every American family.*
II. The result has been that the goal of decent home and suitable environment is still as far distant as ever for the disadvantaged urban family.
III. In spite of this action by Congress, federal housing programs have continued to be fragmented and grossly underfunded.
IV. The passage of the National Housing Act signalled a new federal commitment to provide housing for the nation's citizens.

The CORRECT answer is:

A. I, IV, III, II
B. IV, I, III, II
C. IV, I, II, III
D. II, IV, I, III

15.
I. The greater expense does not necessarily involve *exploitation,* but it is often perceived as exploitative and unfair by those who are aware of the price differences involved, but unaware of operating costs.
II. Ghetto residents believe they are *exploited* by local merchants, and evidence substantiates some of these beliefs.
III. However, stores in low-income areas were more likely to be small independents, which could not achieve the economies available to supermarket chains and were, therefore, more likely to charge higher prices, and the customers were more likely to buy smaller-sized packages which are more expensive per unit of measure.
IV. A study conducted in one city showed that distinctly higher prices were charged for goods sold in ghetto stores than in other areas.

The CORRECT answer is:

A. IV, II, I, III
B. IV, I, III, II
C. II, IV, III, I
D. II, III, IV, I

15.____

KEY (CORRECT ANSWERS)

1. C
2. E
3. B
4. D
5. D

6. C
7. A
8. B
9. C
10. D

11. D
12. C
13. B
14. B
15. C

PREPARING WRITTEN MATERIAL
EXAMINATION SECTION

DIRECTIONS: The following groups of sentences need to be arranged so that the entire passage is correctly organized from start to finish. Select the letter preceding the sequence that represents the best sentence order. *PRINT THE LETTER OF THE CORRECT ANSWER IN THE SPACE AT THE RIGHT.*

Question 1

1._____

1. A large Naval station on Alameda Island, near Oakland, held many warships in port, and the War Department was worried that if the bridge were to be blown up by the enemy, passage to and from the bay would be hopelessly blocked.

2. Though many skeptics were opposed to the idea of building such an enormous bridge, the most vocal opposition came from a surprising source: the United States War Department.

3. The War Department's concerns led to a showdown at San Francisco City Hall between Strauss and the Secretary of War, who demanded to know what would happen if a military enemy blew up the bridge.

4. In 1933, by submitting a construction cost estimate of $17 million, an engineer named Joseph Strauss won the contract to build the Golden Gate Bridge of San Francisco, which would then become one of the world's largest bridges.

5. Strauss quickly ended the debate by explaining that the Golden Gate Bridge was to be a suspension bridge, whose roadway would hang in the air from cables strung between two huge towers, and would immediately sink into three hundred feet of water if it were destroyed.

The best order is
A. 2 3 1 4 5
B. 1 2 3 5 4
C. 4 2 1 3 5
D. 4 1 3 5 2

Question 2 2._____

1. Plastic surgeons have already begun to use virtual reality to map out the complex nerve and tissue structures of a particular patient's face, in order to prepare for delicate surgery.

2. A virtual reality program responds to these movements by adjusting the images that a person sees on a screen or through goggles, thereby creating an "interactive" world in which a person can see and touch three-dimensional graphic objects.

3. No more than a computer program that is designed to build and display graphic images, the virtual reality program takes graphic programs a step further by sensing a person's head and body movements.

4. The computer technology known as virtual reality, now in its very first stages of development, is already revolutionizing some aspects of contemporary life.

5. Virtual reality computers are also being used by the space program, most recently to simulate conditions for the astronauts who were launched on a repair mission to the Hubble telescope.

The best order is
A. 4 2 1 5 3
B. 3 1 5 2 4
C. 4 3 2 1 5
D. 3 1 2 4 5

Question 3 3._____

1. Before you plant anything, the soil in your plant bed should be carefully raked level, a small section at a time, and any clods or rocks that can't be broken up should be removed.

2. Your plant should be placed in a hole that will position it at the same level it was at the nursery, and a small indentation should be pressed into the soil around the plant in order to hold water near it roots.

3. Before placing the plant in the soil, lightly separate any roots that may have been matted together in the container, cutting away any thick masses that can't be separated, so that the remaining roots will be able to grow outward.

4. After the bed is ready, remove your plant from its container by turning it upside down and tapping or pushing on the bottom – never remove it by pulling on the plant.

5. When you bring home a small plant in an individual container from the nursery, there are several things to remember while preparing to plant it in your own garden.

The best order is
A. 5 4 3 2 1
B. 5 1 4 3 2
C. 1 4 2 3 5
D. 1 4 5 2 3

Question 4 4._____

1. The motte and its tower were usually built first, so that sentries could use it as a lookout to warn the castle workers of any danger that might approach the castle.

2. Though the moat and palisade offered the bailey a good deal of protection, it was linked to the motte by a set of stairs that led to a retractable drawbridge at the motte's gate, to enable people to evacuate and retreat onto the motte in case of an attack.

3. The *motte* of these early castles was a fortified hill, sometimes as high as one hundred feet, on which stood a palisade and tower.

4. The *bailey* was a clear, level spot below the motte, also enclosed by a palisade, which in turn was surrounded by a large trench or moat.

5. The earliest castles built in Europe were not the magnificent stone giants that still tower over much of the European landscape, but simpler wooden constructions called motte-and-bailey castles.

The best order is
   A. 5 3 1 4 2
   B. 5 4 1 2 3
   C. 1 4 3 2 5
   D. 1 3 2 4 5

Question 5 5._____

1. If an infant is left alone or abandoned for a short while, its immediate response is to cry loudly, accompanying its screams with aggressive flailing of its legs and limbs.

2. If a child has been abandoned for a longer period of time, it becomes completely still and quiet, as if realizing that now its only chance for survival is to shut its mouth and remain motionless.

3. Along with their intense fear of the dark, the crying behavior of human infants offers insights into how prehistoric newborn children might have evolved instincts that would prevent them from becoming victims of predators.

4. This behavior often surprises people who enter a hospital's maternity ward for the first time and encounter total silence from a roomful of infants.

5. This violent screaming response is quite different from an infant's cries of discomfort or hunger, and seems to serve as either the child's first line of defense against an unwanted intruder, or a desperate attempt to communicate its position to the mother.

The best order is
   A. 3 2 4 1 5
   B. 3 1 5 2 4
   C. 1 5 4 2 3
   D. 2 4 1 5 3

Question 6   6._____

1. When two cats meet who are strangers, their first actions and gestures determine who the "dominant" cat will be, at least for the time being.

2. Unlike dogs, cats are typically a solitary animal species who avoid social interaction, but they do display specific social responses to each other upon meeting.

3. This is unlikely, however; before such a point of open hostility is reached, one of the cats will usually take the "submissive" position of crouching down while looking away from the other cat.

4. If a cat desires dominance or sees the other cat as a threat to its territory, it will stare directly at the intruder with a lowered tail.

5. If the other cat responds with a similar gesture, or with the strong defensive posture of an arched back, laid-back ears and raised tail, a fight or chase is likely if neither cat gives in.

The best order is
A. 4 2 1 5 3
B. 1 2 4 5 3
C. 1 4 5 3 2
D. 2 1 4 5 3

Question 7   7._____

1. A star or planet's gravitational force can best be explained in this way: anything passing through this "dent" in space will veer toward the star or planet as if it were rolling into a hole.

2. Objects that are massive or heavy, such as stars or planets, "sink" into this surface, creating a sort of dent or concavity in the surrounding space.

3. Black holes, the most massive objects known to exist in space, create dents so large and deep that the space surrounding them actually folds in on itself, preventing anything that falls in – even light – from ever escaping again.

4. The sort of dent a star or planet makes depends on how massive it is; planets generally have weak gravitational pulls, but stars, which are larger and heavier, make a bigger "dent" that will attract more matter.

5. In outer space, the force of gravity works as if the surrounding space is a soft, flat surface.

The best order is   7._____
A. 3 5 2 1 4
B. 3 4 1 5 2
C. 5 2 1 4 3
D. 1 5 2 4 3

Question 8   8._____

1. Eventually, the society of Kyoto gave the world one of its first and greatest novels when Japan's most prominent writer, Lady Murasaki Shikibu, wrote her chronicle of Kyoto's society, *The Tale of Genji*, which preceded the first European novels by more than 500 years.

2. The society of Kyoto was dedicated to the pleasures of art; the courtiers experimented with new and colorful methods of sculpture, painting, writing, decorative gardening, and even making clothes.

3. Japanese culture began under the powerful authority of Chinese Buddhism, which influenced every aspect of Japanese life from religion to politics and art.

4. This new, vibrant culture was so sophisticated that all the people in Kyoto's imperial court considered themselves poets, and the line between life and art hardly existed – lovers corresponded entirely through written verses, and even government officials communicated by writing poems to each other.

5. In the eighth century, when the emperor established the town of Kyoto as the capital of the Japanese empire, Japanese society began to develop its own distinctive style.

   The best order is
   A. 5 2 4 1 3
   B. 2 1 5 4 3
   C. 5 3 4 1 2
   D. 3 5 2 4 1

Question 9   9._____

1. Instead of wheels, the HSST uses two sets of magnets, one which sits on the track, and another that is carried by the train; these magnets generate an identical magnetic field which forces the two sets apart.

2. In the last few decades, railway travel has become less popular throughout the world, because it is much slower than travel by airplane, and not much less expensive.

3. The HSST's designers say that the train can take passengers from one town to another as quickly as a jet plane – while consuming less than half the energy.

4. This repellent effect is strong enough to lift the entire train above the trackway, and the train, literally traveling on air, rockets along at speeds of up to 300 miles per hour.

5. The revolutionary technology of magnetic levitation, currently being tested by Japan's experimental HSST (High Speed Surface Transport), may yet bring passenger trains back from the dead.

   The best order is
   A. 2 5 1 4 3
   B. 2 1 4 3 5
   C. 5 2 3 1 4
   D. 5 1 3 4 2

Question 10 10._____

1. When European countries first began to colonize the African continent, their impression of the African people was of a vast group of loosely organized tribal societies, without any great centralized source of power or wealth.

2. The legend of Timbuktu persisted until the nineteenth century, when a French adventurer visited Timbuktu and found that raids by neighboring tribesmen had made the city a shadow of its former self.

3. In the fifteenth century, when the stories of travelers who had traveled Africa's Sudan region began circulating around Europe, this impression began to change.

4. In 1470, an Italian merchant named Benedetto Dei traveled to Timbuktu and confirmed these rumors, describing a thriving metropolis where rich and poor people worshipped together in the city's many ornate mosques – there was even a university in Timbuktu, much like its European counterparts, where African scholars pursued their studies in the arts and sciences.

5. The travelers' legends told of an enormous city in the western Sudan, Timbuktu, where the streets were crowded with goods brought by faraway caravans, and where there was a stone palace as large as any in Europe.

The best order is
A. 3 5 1 4 2
B. 1 2 4 3 5
C. 1 3 5 4 2
D. 2 1 3 4 5

Question 11 11._____

1. Also, our reference points in sighting the moon may make us believe that its size is changing; when the moon is rising through the trees, it seems huge, because our brains unconsciously compare the size of the moon with the size of the trees in the foreground.

2. To most people, the sky itself appears more distant at the horizon than directly overhead, and if the moon's size – which remains constant – is projected from the horizon, the apparent distance of the horizon makes the moon look bigger.

3. Up higher in the sky, the moon is set against tiny stars in the background, which will make the moon seem smaller.

4. People often wonder why the moon becomes bigger when it approaches the horizon, but most scientists agree that this is a complicated optical illusion, produced by at least three factors.

5. The moon illusion may also be partially explained by a phenomenon that has nothing to do with errors in our perception – light that enters the earth's atmosphere is sometimes refracted, and so the atmosphere may act as a kind of magnifying glass for the moon's image.

The best order is
A. 4 3 5 2 1
B. 4 2 1 3 5
C. 5 2 1 3 4
D. 2 1 3 4 5

Question 12   12._____

1. When the Native Americans were introduced to the horses used by white explorers, they were amazed at their new alternative – here was an animal that was strong and swift, would patiently carry a person or other loads on its back, and, they later discovered, was right at home on the plains.

2. Before the arrival of European explorers to North America, the natives of the American plains used large dogs to carry their travois-long lodgepoles loaded with clothing, gear, and food.

3. These horses, it is now known, were not really strangers to North America; the very first horses originated here, on this continent, tens of thousands of years ago, and migrated into Asia across the Bering Land Bridge, a strip of land that used to link our continent with the Eastern world.

4. At first, the natives knew so little about horses that at least one tribe tried to feed their new animals pieces of dried meat and animal fat, and were surprised when the horses turned their heads away and began to eat the grass of the prairie.

5. The American horse eventually became extinct, but its Asian cousins were reintroduced to the New World when the European explorers brought them to live among the Native Americans.

The best order is
A. 2 1 4 3 5
B. 2 4 1 3 5
C. 1 2 4 3 5
D. 1 3 5 2 4

Question 13   13._____

1. The dress worn by the dancer is believed to have been adorned in the past by shells which would strike each other as the dancer performed, creating a lovely sound.

2. Today's jingle-dress is decorated with the tin lids of snuff cans, which are rolled into cones and sewn onto the dress.

3. During the jingle-dress dance, the dancer must blend complicated footwork with a series of gentle hops that cause the cones to jingle in rhythm to a drumbeat.

4. When contemporary Native American tribes meet for a pow-wow, one of the most popular ceremonies to take place is the women's jingle-dress dance.

5. Besides being more readily available than shells, the lids are thought by many dancers to create a softer, more subtle sound.

The best order is
A. 2 4 5 1 3
B. 4 2 1 3 5
C. 2 1 3 5 4
D. 4 1 2 5 3

Question 14   14._____

1. If a homeowner lives where seasonal climates are extreme, deciduous shade trees – which will drop their leaves in the winter and allow sunlight to pass through the windows – should be planted near the southern exposure in order to keep the house cool during the summer.

2. This trajectory is shorter and lower in the sky than at any other time of year during the winter, when a house most requires heating; the northern- facing parts of a house do not receive any direct sunlight at all.

3. In designing an energy-efficient house, especially in colder climates, it is important to remember that most of the house's windows should face south.

4. Though the sun always rises in the east and sets in the west, the sun of the northern hemisphere is permanently situated in the southern portion of the sky.

5. The explanation for why so many architects and builders want this "southern exposure" is related to the path of the sun in the sky.

The best order is
A. 3 1 5 4 2
B. 3 5 4 2 1
C. 1 3 4 2 5
D. 1 2 5 4 3

Question 15   15._____

1. His journeying lasted twenty-four years and took him over an estimated 75,000 miles, a distance that would not be surpassed by anyone other than Magellan – who sailed around the world – for another six hundred years.

2. Perhaps the most far-flung of these lesser-known travelers was Ibn Batuta, an African Moslem who left his birthplace of Tangier in the summer of 1325.

3. Ibn Batuta traveled all over Africa and Asia, from Niger to Peking, and to the islands of Maldive and Indonesia.

4. However, a few explorers of the Eastern world logged enough miles and adventures to make Marco Polo's voyage look like an evening stroll.

5. In America, the most well-known of the Old World's explorers are usually Europeans such as Marco Polo, the Italian who brought many elements of Chinese culture to the Western world.

The best order is
A. 5 4 2 3 1
B. 5 4 3 2 1
C. 3 2 1 4 5
D. 2 3 1 4 5

Question 16   16._____

1. In the rain forests of South America, a rare species of frog practices a reproductive method that is entirely different from this standard process.

2. She will eventually carry each of the tadpoles up into the canopy and drop each into its own little pool, where it will be easy to locate and safe from most predators.

3. After fertilization, the female of the species, who lives almost entirely on the forest floor, lays between 2 and 16 eggs among the leaf litter at the base of a tree, and stands watch over these eggs until they hatch.

4. Most frogs are pond-dwellers who are able to deposit hundreds of eggs in the water and then leave them alone, knowing that enough eggs have been laid to insure the survival of some of their offspring.

5. Once the tadpoles emerge, the female backs in among them, and a tadpole will wriggle onto her back to be carried high into the forest canopy, where the female will deposit it in a little pool of water cupped in the leaf of a plant.

   The best order is
   A. 1 4 3 2 5
   B. 1 3 5 2 4
   C. 4 3 2 5 1
   D. 4 1 3 5 2

Question 17   17._____

1. Eratosthenes had heard from travelers that at exactly noon on June 21, in the ancient city of Aswan, Egypt, the sun cast no shadow in a well, which meant that the sun must be directly overhead.

2. He knew the sun always cast a shadow in Alexandria, and so he figured that if he could measure the length of an Alexandria shadow at the time when there was no shadow in Aswan, he could calculate the angle of the sun, and therefore the circumference of the earth.

3. The evidence for a round earth was not new in 1492; in fact, Eratosthenes, an Alexandrian geographer who lived nearly sixteen centuries before Columbus's voyage (275-195 B.C.), actually developed a method for calculating the circumference of the earth that is still in use today.

4. Eratosthenes's method was correct, but his result – 28,700 miles – was about 15 percent too high, probably because of the inaccurate ancient methods of keeping time, and because Aswan was not due south of Alexandria, as Eratosthenes had believed.

5. When Christopher Columbus sailed across the Atlantic Ocean for the first time in 1492, there were still some people in the world who ignored scientific evidence and believed that the earth was flat, rather than round.

   The best order is
   A. 1 2 5 3 4
   B. 5 3 4 1 2
   C. 5 3 1 2 4
   D. 3 5 1 2 4

Question 18

18._____

1. The first name for the child is considered a trial naming, often impersonal and neutral, such as the Ngoni name *Chabwera*, meaning "it has arrived."

2. This sort of name is not due to any parental indifference to the child, but is a kind of silent recognition of Africa's sometimes high infant death rate; most parents ease the pain of losing a child with the belief that it is not really a person until it has been given a final name.

3. In many tribal African societies, families often give two different names to their children, at different periods in time.

4. After the trial naming period has subsided and it is clear that the child will survive, the parents choose a final name for the child, an act that symbolically completes the act of birth.

5. In fact, some African first-given names are explicitly uncomplimentary, translating as "I am dead" or "I am ugly," in order to avoid the jealousy of ancestral spirits who might wish to take a child that is especially healthy or attractive.

The best order is
A. 3 1 2 5 4
B. 3 4 2 1 5
C. 4 3 1 2 5
D. 4 5 3 1 2

Question 19

19._____

1. Though uncertain of the definite reasons for this behavior, scientists believe the birds digest the clay in order to counteract toxins contained in the seeds of certain fruits that are eaten by macaws.

2. For example, all macaws flock to riverbanks at certain times of the year to eat the clay that is found in river mud.

3. The macaws of South America are not only among the largest and most beautifully colored of the world's flying birds, but they are also one of the smartest.

4. It is believed that macaws are forced to resort to these toxic fruits during the dry season, when foods are more scarce.

5. The macaw's intelligence has led to intense study by scientists, who have discovered some macaw behaviors that have not yet been explained.

The best order is
A. 3 4 1 2 5
B. 3 5 2 1 4
C. 5 2 1 4 3
D. 4 1 2 3 5

Question 20   20._____

1. Although Maggie Kuhn has since passed away, the Gray Panthers are still waging a campaign to reinstate the historical view of the elderly as people whose experience allows them to make their greatest contribution in their later years.

2. In 1972, an elderly woman named Maggie Kuhn responded to this sort of treatment by forming a group called the Gray Panthers, an organization of both old and young adults with the common goal of creating change.

3. This attitude is reflected strongly in the way elderly people are treated by our society; many are forced into early retirement, or are placed in rest homes in which they are isolated from their communities.

4. Unlike most other cultures around the world, Americans tend to look upon old age with a sense of dread and sadness.

5. Kuhn believed that when the elderly are forced to withdraw into lives that lack purpose, society loses one of its greatest resources: people who have a lifetime of experience and wisdom to offer their communities.

The best order is
A. 4 3 2 5 1
B. 4 2 1 3 5
C. 2 4 3 5 1
D. 2 1 4 3 5

Question 21   21._____

1. The current theory among most anthropologists is that humans evolved from apes who lived in trees near the grasslands of Africa.

2. Still, some anthropologists insist that such an invention was necessary for the survival of early humans, and point to the Kung Bushmen of central Africa as a society in which the sling is still used in this way.

3. Two of these inventions – fire, and weapons such as spears and clubs – were obvious defenses against predators, and there is archaeological evidence to support the theory of their use.

4. Once people had evolved enough to leave the safety of trees and walk upright, they needed the protection of several inventions in order to survive.

5. But another invention, a leather or fiber sling that allowed mothers to carry children while leaving their hands free to gather roots or berries, would certainly have decomposed and left behind no trace of itself.

The best order is
A. 1 2 3 5 4
B. 4 1 2 3 5
C. 1 4 3 5 2
D. 4 3 5 2 1

Question 22   22._____

1. The person holding the bird should keep it in hot water up to its neck, and the person cleaning should work a mild solution of dishwashing liquid into the bird's plumage, paying close attention to the head and neck.

2. When rinsing the bird, after all the oil has been removed, the running water should be directed against the lay of its feathers, until water begins to bead off the surface of the feathers – a sign that all the detergent has been rinsed out.

3. If you have rescued a sea bird from an oil spill and want to restore it to clean and normal living, you need a large sink, a constant supply of running hot water (a little over 100° F), and regular dishwashing liquid.

4. This cleaning with detergent solution should be repeated as many times as it takes to remove all traces of oil from the bird's feathers, sometimes over a period of several days.

5. But before you begin to clean the bird, you must first find a partner, because cleaning an oiled bird is a two-person job.

The best order is
A. 3 1 2 4 5
B. 3 5 1 4 2
C. 3 1 4 5 2
D. 3 4 5 1 2

Question 23   23._____

1. The most difficult time of year for the Tsaatang is the spring calving, when the reindeer leave their wintering ground and rush to their accustomed calving place, without stopping by night or by day.

2. Reindeer travel in herds, and though some animals are tamed by the Tsaatang for riding or milking, the herds are allowed to roam free.

3. This journey is hard for the Tsaatang, who carry all their possessions with them, but once it's over it proves worthwhile; the Tsaatang can immediately begin to gather milk from reindeer cows who have given birth.

4. The Tsaatang, a small tribe who live in the far northwest corner of Mongolia, practice a lifestyle that is completely dependent on the reindeer, their main resource for food, clothing, and transport.

5. The people must follow their yearly migrations, living in portable shelters that resemble Native American tepees.

The best order is
A. 1 3 2 5 4
B. 1 4 2 5 3
C. 4 1 3 5 2
D. 4 2 5 1 3

Question 24   24._____

1. The Romans later improved this system by installing these heated pipe networks throughout walls and ceilings, supplying heat to even the uppermost floors of a building – a system that, to this day, hasn't been much improved.

2. Air-conditioning, the method by which humans control indoor temperatures, was practiced much earlier than most people think.

3. The earliest heating devices other than open fires were used in 350 B.C. by the ancient Greeks, who directed air that had been heated by underground fires into baked clay pipes that ran under the floor.

4. Ironically, the first successful cooling system, patented in England in 1831, used fire as its main energy source – fires were lit in the attic of a building, creating an updraft of air that drew cool air into the building through ducts that had underground openings near the river Thames.

5. Cooling buildings was more of a challenge, and wasn't attempted until 1500: a water-based system, designed by Leonardo da Vinci, does not appear to have been successful, since it was never used again.

   The best order is
   A. 3 5 4 1 2
   B. 3 1 2 5 4
   C. 2 3 1 5 4
   D. 4 2 3 1 5

Question 25   25._____

1. Cold, dry air from Canada passes over the Rocky Mountains and sweeps down onto the plains, where it collides with warm, moist air from the waters of the Gulf of Mexico, and when the two air masses meet, the resulting disturbance sometimes forms a violent funnel cloud that strikes the earth and destroys virtually everything in its path.

2. Hurricanes, storms which are generally not this violent and last much longer, are usually given names by meteorologists, but this tradition cannot be applied to tornados, which have a life span measured in minutes and disappear in the same way as they are born – unnamed.

3. A tornado funnel forms rotating columns of air whose speed reaches three hundred miles and hour – a speed that can only be estimated, because no wind-measuring devices in the direct path of a storm have ever survived.

4. The natural phenomena known as tornados occur primarily over the midwestern grasslands of the United States.

5. It is here, meteorologists tell us, that conditions for the formation of tornados are sometimes perfect during the spring months.

   The best order is
   A. 2 4 5 1 3
   B. 2 3 1 5 4
   C. 4 5 1 3 2
   D. 4 3 1 5 2

KEY (CORRECT ANSWERS)

1. C	11. B	21. C
2. C	12. A	22. B
3. B	13. D	23. D
4. A	14. B	24. C
5. B	15. A	25. C
6. D	16. D	
7. C	17. C	
8. D	18. A	
9. A	19. B	
10. C	20. A	

ANSWER SHEET

TEST NO. _____ PART _____ TITLE OF POSITION _____

(AS GIVEN IN EXAMINATION ANNOUNCEMENT - INCLUDE OPTION, IF ANY)

PLACE OF EXAMINATION _____ DATE _____

(CITY OR TOWN)   (STATE)

RATING

USE THE SPECIAL PENCIL. MAKE GLOSSY BLACK MARKS.

Make only ONE mark for each answer. Additional and stray marks may be counted as mistakes. In making corrections, erase errors COMPLETELY.

MAY – – 2016

ANSWER SHEET

TEST NO. _____ PART _____ TITLE OF POSITION _____
(AS GIVEN IN EXAMINATION ANNOUNCEMENT - INCLUDE OPTION, IF ANY)

PLACE OF EXAMINATION _____ DATE _____
(CITY OR TOWN)   (STATE)

RATING

USE THE SPECIAL PENCIL.   MAKE GLOSSY BLACK MARKS.

Make only ONE mark for each answer.   Additional and stray marks may be counted as mistakes.   In making corrections, erase errors COMPLETELY.